Career Planning
and Job Searching
in the Information Age

Forthcoming topics in *The Reference Librarian* series:

• Archives and Reference Services, Number 56

Published:

Career Planning and Job Searching in the Information Age has also been published as *The Reference Librarian*, Number 55 1996.

Reprinted 2009 by CRC Press

The Haworth Press, Inc., 10 Alice Street, Binghamton, NY 13904-1580 USA

Library of Congress Cataloging-in-Publication Data

Career planning and job searching in the information age / Elizabeth Lorenzen, editor.
    p. cm.
    "Has also been published as The reference librarian, number 55, 1996"–T.p. verso.
    Includes bibliographical references.
    ISBN 1-56024-838-6 (alk. paper)
    1. Vocational guidance–Information services. 2. Job hunting–Information services. 3. Reference services (Libraries) 4. Internet (Computer network) 5. Information storage and retrieval systems–Vocational guidance. I. Lorenzen, Elizabeth.
HF5381.C2665 1996   96-20566
025.06'331702–dc20   CIP

Career Planning and Job Searching in the Information Age

Elizabeth A. Lorenzen
Editor

CRC Press
Taylor & Francis Group
Boca Raton   London   New York

CRC Press is an imprint of the
Taylor & Francis Group, an informa business

INDEXING & ABSTRACTING

Contributions to this publication are selectively indexed or abstracted in print, electronic, online, or CD-ROM version(s) of the reference tools and information services listed below. This list is current as of the copyright date of this publication. See the end of this section for additional notes.

- *Academic Abstracts/CD-ROM,* EBSCO Publishing, P.O. Box 2250, Peabody, MA 01960-7250

- *Academic Search: data base of 2,000 selected academic serials. updated monthly:* EBSCO Publishing, 83 Pine Street, Peabody, MA 10960

- *CNPIEC Reference Guide: Chinese National Directory of Foreign Periodicals,* P.O. Box 88, Beijing, People's Republic of China

- *Current Awareness Bulletin,* Association for Information Management, Information House, 20-24 Old Street, London EC1V 9AP, England

- *Current Index to Journals in Education,* Syracuse University, 4-194 Center for Science and Technology, Syracuse, NY 13244-4100

- *Educational Administration Abstracts (EAA),* Sage Publications, Inc., 2455 Teller Road, Newbury Park, CA 91320

- *IBZ International Bibliography of Periodical Literature,* Zeller Verlag GmbH & Co., P.O.B. 1949, d-49009 Osnabruck, Germany

- *Index to Periodical Articles Related to Law,* University of Texas, 727 East 26th Street, Austin, TX 78705

- *Information Science Abstracts,* Plenum Publishing Company, 233 Spring Street, New York, NY 10013-1578

- *Informed Librarian, The,* Infosources Publishing, 140 Norma Road, Teaneck, NJ 07666

- *INSPEC Information Services,* Institution of Electrical Engineers, Michael Faraday House, Six Hills Way, Stevenage, Herts SG1 2AY, England

(continued)

- *INTERNET ACCESS (& additional networks) Bulletin Board for Libraries ("BUBL"), coverage of information resources on INTERNET, JANET, and other networks.*
  - JANET X.29: UK.AC.BATH.BUBL or 00006012101300
  - TELNET: BUBL.BATH.AC.UK or 138.38.32.45 login 'bubl'
  - Gopher: BUBL.BATH.AC.UK (138.32.32.45). Port 7070
  - World Wide Web: http: / / www.bubl.bath.ac.uk./BUBL/ home.html
  - NISSWAIS: telnetniss.ac.uk (for the NISS gateway)

  The Andersonian Library, Curran Building, 101 St. James Road, Glasgow G4 ONS, Scotland

- *Konyvtari Figyelo-Library Review,* National Sczechnyi Library, Centre for Library and Information Science, H-1827 Budapest, Hungary

- *Library & Information Science Abstracts (LISA),* Bowker-Saur Limited, Maypole House, Maypole Road, East Grinstead, West Sussex, RH19 1HH England

- *Library Literature,* The H.W. Wilson Company, 950 University Avenue, Bronx, NY 10452

- *MasterFILE: updated database from EBSCO Publishing,* EBSCO Publishing, 83 Pine Street, Peabody, MA 01960

- *Newsletter of Library and Information Services,* China Sci-Tech Book Review, Library of Academia Sinica, 8 Kexueyuan Nanlu, Zhongguancun, Beijing 100080, People's Republic of China

- *OT BibSys,* American Occupational Therapy Foundation, P.O. Box 31220, Bethesda, MD 20824-1220

- *Referativnyi Zhurnal (Abstracts Journal of the Institute of Scientific Information of the Republic of Russia),* The Institute of Scientific Information, Baltijskaja ul., 14, Moscow A-219, Republic of Russia

- *Sage Public Administration Abstracts (SPAA),* Sage Publications, Inc., 2455 Teller Road, Newbury Park, CA 91320

(continued)

SPECIAL BIBLIOGRAPHIC NOTES

related to special journal issues (separates)
and indexing/abstracting

☐ indexing/abstracting services in this list will also cover material in any "separate" that is co-published simultaneously with Haworth's special thematic journal issue or DocuSerial. Indexing/abstracting usually covers material at the article/chapter level.

☐ monographic co-editions are intended for either non-subscribers or libraries which intend to purchase a second copy for their circulating collections.

☐ monographic co-editions are reported to all jobbers/wholesalers/approval plans. The source journal is listed as the "series" to assist the prevention of duplicate purchasing in the same manner utilized for books-in-series.

☐ to facilitate user/access services all indexing/abstracting services are encouraged to utilize the co-indexing entry note indicated at the bottom of the first page of each article/chapter/contribution.

☐ this is intended to assist a library user of any reference tool (whether print, electronic, online, or CD-ROM) to locate the monographic version if the library has purchased this version but not a subscription to the source journal.

☐ individual articles/chapters in any Haworth publication are also available through the Haworth Document Delivery Services (HDDS).

Career Planning and Job Searching in the Information Age

CONTENTS

V. ACCESS ISSUES

ABOUT THE EDITOR

Elizabeth A. Lorenzen, MLS, is the Career Center Librarian at Indiana State University in Terre Haute, Indiana. Besides having authored several articles about career resources, libraries, and the job search, her other research interests lie in the ethical use of electronic information and collection development on the Internet. Correspondence is welcomed through her email address: CARLORE@STSERV.INDSTATE.EDU

I. INTRODUCTION/THE ISSUES

The Librarian's Role
in the Job Search of the Future:
Issues and Ethics
in the Electronic Environment

Elizabeth A. Lorenzen

CHANGES IN WORKFORCE PARADIGMS

When this editor first approached Byron Anderson, guest editor of the *Reference Librarian* volume entitled "Library Services for Career Planning, Job Searching, and Employment Opportunities," about the possibility of a follow-up book, it was very much agreed how important it was, and also thematically what the volume should contain. The impact of the Internet and other forms of electronic information delivery upon the way individuals conduct their job searches is deepening daily. Also, as the Internet becomes increas-

Elizabeth A. Lorenzen is the Career Center Librarian at Indiana State University in Terre Haute, IN. See "About the Guest Editor."

[Haworth co-indexing entry note]: "The Librarian's Role in the Job Search of the Future: Issues and Ethics in the Electronic Environment." Lorenzen, Elizabeth A. Co-published simultaneously in *The Reference Librarian* (The Haworth Press, Inc.) No. 55, 1996, pp. 1-6; and: *Career Planning and Job Searching in the Information Age* (ed: Elizabeth A. Lorenzen) The Haworth Press, Inc., 1996, pp. 1-6. Single or multiple copies of this article are available from The Haworth Document Delivery Service [1-800-342-9678, 9:00 a.m. - 5:00 p.m. (EST). E-mail address: getinfo@haworth.com].

© 1996 by The Haworth Press, Inc. All rights reserved.

ingly commercialized, it is having a profound effect upon the way that employers communicate; between each other, the customers they serve, and even prospective employees.

Indeed, as the Information Age dares to go where no one has gone before, the change that comes with it is altering radically the world's view of work. A society that basically has been industrial for the past two hundred years is now shifting gears dramatically and viewing the world through the eyes of a knowledge-based society; that is, one that is information oriented, with a workforce evaluated by current skill sets instead of career paths and chronological work histories. At the same time, librarians are being challenged within their own profession to take a hard look at the ways that they find, evaluate, and disseminate information. They are also being challenged to learn new and creative ways to effectively instruct others to do the same.

Placing these concepts within the context of career planning and the job search throws light on an added dimension to all of these issues. While librarians are reevaluating their places within a profession that is experiencing a great deal of change, the changes going on in the "world of work," which affect how individuals plan for careers and seek employment, are placing new levels of expectation upon librarians, who have long been traditional providers of career information to their clientele.

Now more than ever, librarians who are striving to meet the career information needs of their constituents must consider the fact that as access to electronic job search information grows, there will be a greater need to target carefully information for clients. They also need to take into consideration the stage of the career development process in which they are engaged. This process is essential in order to be able literally to wade through the information that is available. Anyone who has spent any time at all on the Internet can attest to this; and librarians will need to work more closely than ever with career counselors regarding the interpretation of information needs of clients. It is a concern of this author that as more and more information becomes readily available to individuals online without necessarily having to work with a career counselor to obtain it, to what level will librarians be asked by clients to aid in the interpretation of information? This is not an easy question to be answered, and one with ethical implications, to be sure; but needless to say, as librarians are called upon to help their clients create effective search strategies in order to target the most relevant information for their job searches and other career exploration activities, these questions may arise, and librarians will more than ever need to develop good working relationships with career counselors whenever possible in order to best meet these needs.

ENTER THE INTERNET AND INFORMATION AGE

The very characteristics that make up the nature of the Internet make it both a wealthy source of current information and a frustrating resource when attempting to verify its reliability. While it is possible to find employment information on the Net that is minutes old, it can also be difficult to ascertain authorship, how often the information is updated, and other standards that librarians have traditionally used to judge the reliability of resources. There is also, at the time of the writing of this article, no clear law regarding the interpretation of copyright legislation in regards to the Internet. Lack of all of these standards causes one rightfully to question the reliability of the Internet as an effective reference tool for career development and the job search. Therefore, one of the main purposes of this volume, particularly through the articles that serve as Internet resource guides, is to begin to establish reliability and integrity of resources that have proven their stability through regular use, so that librarians who are just learning to use job search information on the Internet have some sort of benchmark from which to begin their own investigative efforts.

The changeability of the Internet made this project somewhat daunting at the onset. The authors whose articles focused on Internet resources were quite concerned about the timeliness of the volume, fearing that because the Internet is changing so constantly, their sources would become quickly outdated and contain incorrect information by the time of printing. In order to maintain the integrity of the publication, it was the responsibility of the editor to make sure that sources listed were as stable and dependable to use as possible. Also, Internet addresses were checked for correctness up to the last moment to ensure the accuracy of the resources being listed.

CAREER INFORMATION RESOURCE DEVELOPMENT STRATEGIES FOR THE REFERENCE LIBRARIAN

As many resources on conducting an effective job search can attest, the concept of networking is seen as the single most effective tool that any person can use in order to develop professionally. Regularly communicating with a circle of colleagues is the ticket, not only to keep up with current trends, but employment opportunities as well. In the Information Age, the plethora of available information is so great that it would be impossible for any one librarian to consistently be apprised of not only what information is available, but the quality and reliability of it. Through networking, librarians can exchange information about such issues electronically and keep updated concerning new resources and their access daily. JCIS-L, an electronic forum for librarians interested in job and career information services, and JOBPLACE, a forum for career development professionals, could facilitate this process over the Internet, and this author encourages librarians to use this technique in order to attempt to keep a handle on the fast paced changes that are taking place in the realm of electronic career and job search information.

To use this volume more effectively as a guide, two appendices were developed which cite all journal references in a comprehensive format. The first lists all Internet addresses (URLs) for the Internet resources that are discussed so that readers have ready, easy access to these references when developing their own Internet tools and guides. The second appendix is a comprehensive bibliography that should serve as a good basis for additional reading and collection development purposes. If any reader has any problems or questions regarding these resources, he/she should not hesitate to contact the corresponding authors. It is through this type of cooperative resource development work that the effectiveness and integrity of our services as information providers in a virtual environment can be maintained.

CONCLUSION

As this author looks back on all of the work that has taken place toward the development of this volume, it is amazing to see the impact that the Internet had on her abilities as an editor to work with all of the authors who collaborated on this project. Through the Internet there was an exchange of ideas, manuscript drafts, and other publication details that could not have been facilitated more easily, or in a more timely fashion. In retrospect, the volume may have been more well rounded if additional articles from career development professionals could have been added, for their own professional perspectives are so valuable to librarians. More information on international employment and services to other special groups would have been helpful also. Maybe these topics could be covered through yet another successive volume! All in all, the volume has a focus on the Internet, but provides other information on instructional issues, services to certain demographic groups, and presents some topics relating to information access that are of concern to librarians and career development professionals alike.

Special thanks go to Byron Anderson for his encouragement and support regarding taking on the project. His insight and advice regarding editorial responsibilities was invaluable and made a big difference throughout the execution of these duties. Finally, highest regards go to Bill Katz for his positive feedback and wonderful sense of humor, which had quite a calming effect when authors were disappearing from sight and there was so much worry about deadlines. His insistence that quality, not quantity, was the focus was quite encouraging.

In conclusion, again, the author would very much like to encourage communication from any reader with questions and concerns regarding the volume or any ideas about career resources and libraries. Personal experience is the best teacher of all, but sharing it is the best gift.

BIBLIOGRAPHY

Anderson, Byron. *Library Services For Career Planning, Job Searching and Employment Opportunities.* New York: The Haworth Press, Inc., 1992.

Arnold, Steven. "Relationships of the Future: Vendors and Partners." *Special Libraries,* Fall 1993, p. 235-240.

Durrance, Joan. "Kellogg Funded Education and Career Information Centers in Public Libraries." *Journal of Career Development,* Vol. 18(1), Fall 1991, p. 11-17.

Herr, Edwin L.; Rayman, Jack R.; and Garis, Jeffrey W. *Handbook For the College and University Career Center.* Westport, CT: Greenwood Press, 1992.

Hogeveen, Eunice and Jones, Rebecca. "Paradox, Paragon, or Paralysis?: Three Organizations in 2005." *Special Libraries,* Fall 1993, p. 220-225.

Howland, Pat and Palmer, Ray. "Ethics and Computer Guidance: Uneasy Partners?" *Journal of Career Planning and Employment,* Summer 1992, p. 38-45.

Mallinger, Stephen Mark. "Workplace: Linking Career Counselors and Librarians in Pennsylvania." *Journal of Career Development,* Vol. 18(1), Fall 1991, p. 31-36.

Ojala, Marydee. "What Will They Call Us in the Future?" *Special Libraries,* Fall 1993, p. 226-229.

Sampson, James P. "Training Librarians to Deliver Career Services." *Journal of Career Development,* Vol. 18(1), Fall 1991, p. 19-30.

Stahl, Gail. "The Virtual Library: Prospect and Promise." *Special Libraries*, Fall 1993, p. 202-205.

The Internet as Career, Job, and Employment Resource: Transition, Assimilation, Instruction

Byron Anderson

SUMMARY. The Internet is becoming a key player in the provision of career, job, and employment information, though it is still being readied for prime time use. Libraries and career and job services are in a transitional phase that is leading to common use of the Internet. While there is a sense of urgency to jump on the Internet bandwagon, professionals have time to learn and assimilate this new electronic culture. This article presents a broad understanding of Internet development, discusses barriers to both learning and teaching the Internet, offers tips and methods for hurdling these barriers, and briefly describes some of the career job sites currently found on the Internet. *[Article copies available from The Haworth Document Delivery Service: 1-800-342-9678. E-mail address: getinfo@haworth.com]*

INTRODUCTION

You simply can't overstate the significance of the digital transformation of our society.

Nicholas Negroponte
Director, MIT Media Lab

Byron Anderson is Acting Head of Reference, Northern Illinois University Libraries, DeKalb, IL 60115.

[Haworth co-indexing entry note]: "The Internet as Career, Job, and Employment Resource: Transition, Assimilation, Instruction." Anderson, Byron. Co-published simultaneously in *The Reference Librarian* (The Haworth Press, Inc.) No 55, 1996, pp. 7-17; and: *Career Planning and Job Searching in the Information Age* (ed: Elizabeth A. Lorenzen) The Haworth Press, Inc., 1996, pp. 7-17. Single or multiple copies of this article are available from The Haworth Document Delivery Service [1-800-342-9678, 9:00 a.m. - 5:00 p.m. (EST). E-mail address: getinfo@haworth.com].

. . . a bloomin' buzzin' confusion.

—William James

When it comes to information access we, like Dorothy, find we're no longer in Kansas anymore. The Internet is changing the way society recreates, communicates, educates, informs, conducts research, and does business. However, it is still in the initial stages of development, a sort of paleoelectronic era. Librarians and others in career and job services are beginning a transitional phase that is blending the old with the new, leading to common use of electronic information. This transition will take time, money, patience, and new knowledge.

TIMELINE PERSPECTIVES

The Internet seems to be here before its time, sudden and imposing itself on individuals and society. Yet, Internet's history can be traced back 26 years to the origin of ARPAnet, the Department of Defense's answer to keeping communication channels open in case of a national emergency. Along the way, no one could have predicted the scale of today's extensive global networking. By early 1995, more than 60 countries had full use of the Internet and an additional 91 were connected by e-mail. Growth measured by use was increasing 8 to 9 percent a month. The Internet is available to anyone who has a vehicle, an on-ramp, and knows how to drive on the information superhighway. Businesspersons, librarians, educators, students, and those in career planning and job search services are feeling impelled to jump on the Internet bandwagon.

The promise of the Internet as a viable complementary resource tool for career planning and job searching is becoming a reality, but one that is, for the most part, future oriented. There are two timelines that will help put this development into perspective. First, studies have shown that new technologies take approximately twenty to thirty years before they are assimilated by the masses. A good example is the personal computer, first introduced to the public in 1974 with the Altair 8800. Today, thirty-five percent of American households have PCs, and for purposes here, most do not have online access. For the Internet, its exact beginning or introduction is difficult to determine; it is, after all, the blending together of numerous technologies. Most likely, starting dates include either 1986 with the linking of the nation's five super computing centers through the NSFnet, creating the necessary backbone connection, or 1991 with the Congressional passage of the High Performance Computing Act, therefore placing Internet on the national agenda.

Second, though the Internet is growing rapidly, only two percent of the U.S. population currently use it on a regular basis. Mass use of the Internet as an information resource tool (as we know it today) will probably not occur until well into the first decade of the 21st century. For now, most career planners and job seekers are able to proceed adequately in today's job market without using the Internet, though it is adviseable to complement a career plan or job search with Internet resources whenever possible. At the same time, even though individuals have successfully found employment through Internet postings, it is unadvisable to rely on just the Internet to find employment. Using the Internet at this time will serve, at the very least, as groundwork for the future. In other words, librarians and career/job professionals should get connected, get comfortable with the applications, and stay current with changes, even though it may be some time before the Internet provides consistent and stable resources offering comprehensive and reliable information. How do librarians and career/job professionals handle this transition and assimilate the use of the Internet into their current work with clients?

LEARNING: BARRIERS AND BENEFITS

Like it or not, librarians and other career and job professionals are going to have to find the wherewithal to make sense of the chaos that is in the Internet. When considering the Internet, those in career planning and job searching services need to ask many questions, but foremost in their minds should be to ask themselves what the Net has to offer, and how it can help reach professional goals, as well as the goals of career planners and job seekers. The answers will vary, but first the Internet must be learned. To learn, one should proceed with the following understanding:

a. Learning the Internet is a time-consuming process;
b. The Internet is an evolving system and changes are common;

   c. Technostress is part of the learning;

   d. Some individuals will require an attitude adjustment before they will be able to absorb Internet culture;

   e. The Internet is presenting as much promise for a better future as it is presenting challenges to today's society;

   f. In most instances, it will take many years before traditional information resources and work procedures are integrated with Internet utilities;

   g. The Internet is maturing, but not ready for prime time use in many professional disciplines.

The Internet is in transition; however, transitional issues today may be taken for granted ten or twenty years from now. For now, how well individuals assimilate and how much society benefits from the Internet remains to be seen.

Learning the Internet requires that one hurdle many barriers, starting with a basic understanding of what is available on the Internet and how to access it. Many librarians and career and job resource professionals, and moreover the patrons they serve, are at ground-zero, that is, they may be able to find the "on-switch" but not the "on-ramp." Complicating this is the rapid evolution of information technology, one that requires more power in a personal computer and new knowledge. Because of this, and the sheer volume and growth of information, one can be easily overwhelmed in the learning process.

It has been suggested that for every dollar spent on technology a dollar should be spent on training (Peck, 1994). Few libraries, if any, can afford this, and as a result remain unable to provide proper Internet training for either staff or patrons. Most often, individuals learn the Internet on a catch-as-catch-can basis. What is really needed is to have librarians return to the classroom for course work, or work one-on-one with a knowledgeable colleague, but time and money normally prevent this from happening. How does one become competent in the Internet?

Learning the Internet often proceeds step-by-step through its main applications. However, some basic groundwork is necessary before delving into the applications. The most basic question is, what is the Internet? While often defined amorphously, such as a network of networks, the Internet is so ubiquitous and peripatetic as to defy definition. For one, it is developing more rapidly in the directions of business and entertainment than in education and research. Educational resources, including career planning and job searching information, are on the Internet and will continue to grow, but they're a small part of the total picture. Career and job sites share cyberspace with a great deal of other types of information, most of which is unmoderated, e.g., neo-Nazi newsgroups (Kilian, 1994). Career planners and job searchers will need direction through this maze of information, and librarians are among the few professions that are publically placed to offer this instruction.

Another barrier to be tackled is the entry-level vocabulary. Internet operations trap users in a field that is laced with engineering terms and futurist outlooks. A basic jargon must be incorporated into one's vocabulary as the terms are part of the learning. Examples abound, but for instance, the World Wide Web is associated with homepages, hypertext links, and browsers, such as Mosaic, Netscape, and Cello. Another example is "URL," or Uniform Resource Locator, used to locate information based on addresses, generally arranged protocol://system.domain/pathname/filename. There are many more examples, but building a personal glossary of these terms will greatly aid in learning.

A final barrier to be surmounted before learning the applications is to develop some understanding of connectivity. There are many on-ramps to the Internet, and what a librarian needs know about connectivity will vary from one work situation to another. However, some knowledge of direct and dial-in connections is useful. Direct connections to the Internet are generally associated with businesses and institutions. Direct connections are faster and can do more, but cost more. Individual users will likely have a dial-in access, though SLIP (Serial Line Internet Protocol) or PPP (Point to Point Protocol) software can greatly aid in this. There are many variations to dial-in access. For example, a user can dial in to their company's or institution's computer, to a private carrier, such as America Online, or to a freenet, all of which have, in turn, a direct Internet connection. Knowledge of the various connections will aid professionals in directing patrons to their options for access.

At a base level, it is also useful to understand that Internet access requires an account, and accounts provide the passwords necessary to connect. One does not automatically "get" on the Internet, though public site access is becoming more common. Internet accounts are not free. Even if access is free to a user group, someone pays. Some businesses and institutions have established connections that grant access to their member community, and some freenets allow access to a defined clientele. Persons outside of these groups will likely have to turn to private vendors, such as CompuServe, for access.

INTERNET RESOURCES

Once groundwork for understanding the Internet has been established, the next step is to learn the Internet's main applications. The best way to start is by thoroughly learning the various uses of e-mail. There are enormous professional advantages to having an e-mail address. First, there is one-on-one correspondence with colleagues or clients (assuming that they have an e-mail address), regardless of their location. Second, there are group discussions through listservs and bulletin board systems, many on career and job related topics. One example is *JobPlace*, a discussion group that provides career/job professionals with a network to ask questions and share information. There are "send only" listservs that periodically mail to subscribers relevant topic-related information. Listservs may also store and make available archival files. Finally, e-mail can serve as the utility for receiving electronic journals and newsletters subscribed to online, many free. One way to learn what's available is to check the current edition of the *Directory of Electronic Journals, Newsletters and Academic Discussion Lists* (Washington, DC: Association of Research Libraries, Office of Scientific and Academic Publishing, annual), or on the Internet at listserv@uottawa.ca, send two separate messages: *send ejourn11 directry* and *send ejourn12 directry.*

Beyond e-mail, practical applications move toward access of remote sites. Knowing what's on the Net is one of the biggest problems, and unfortunately, there is a general lack of organization. The Internet has been defined as a gigantic library without a card catalog. However, much effort is being put into organizing Internet resources, and the future looks brighter. Organizing information is one of the areas where librarians have skills, and these can be applied to the Internet. Diane Kovacs is one such person. A librarian at Kent State, she has put together a number of subject-based Gopher menus, including the *Jobs, Employment, Placement Services and Programs* site. Also worthy of note is the Gopher site *Careers, Jobs, Employment* and *JobNet* which not only has job postings but also a Career Resource Manual on tips in seeking employment. For more detail on these and other sites, see the June 1995 issue of *NetGuide*, pages 87-91.

Looking at the examples above will show the good news (it's under one umbrella), and the bad news (it's still bits and pieces). For example, under the Kovacs site, there are fourteen listings. Most of the entries are in specific opportunities, such as international jobs, random occupations, such as aviation, certain groups, such as people with disabilities, and limited geographic areas, such as New York State. Though lacking comprehensiveness, gopher sites like these often grow, and one could argue that the information complements other traditional career plan and job search sources.

There is a strong trend on the Internet towards the posting of job and recruitment information. However, availability of this information may vary from one user to another. For example, private carriers, such as CompuServe or America Online, make available career and job information to their subscribers only. Other job resources are available to those who have access to Usenet. Others may not have World Wide Web access. Overall, the above is saying that not all Internet access is equal or similar.

Another popular trend developing on the Internet is to use personal URLs to publish resumes where, in turn, prospective employers can look at a person's qualifications in multimedia formats. Such URLs can include a resume, photograph, and examples of the applicant's work. Conversely, some companies are posting job openings on their URLs. Then, it's just a matter of key strokes to drop a company a note, telling its personnel officers where to locate a personal URL and resume. One variation of this is JCI Job Canada out of Toronto, a nationwide register that charges potential employees $25 to place their resume on their Internet site, and employers $7 for each resume they order. Searches are done according to the job skill requirements of the work.

One of the most visited sites on the entire Internet is the *Online Career Center*, with over two million accesses per month. It is a database of 10,000-12,000 job listings, and there are also job ad templates available for use and resume databases (Booker, 1994). The Online Career Center is a gophering menu system that provides for searches both by area and occupation. Additionally, it allows a user to post resumes, through e-mail, at no cost.

The final main application of the Internet is ftp, or file transfer protocol. File transfer can provide a great deal of information, much of it in the public domain stored in remote computers. It is available for transfer to personal computers, but accessing and downloading this information is more difficult than other applications. In ftp, there are both ASCII and binary files, as well as compressed files that need to be unzipped. To accomplish this requires more knowledge than other applications; however, with patience and good instruction, ftp can be learned. As more and more information moves to an electronic format, file transfer will come to play an increasingly important role in information and document delivery, and librarians will be one of the main facilitators in this process.

The listing of career, employment and job resources on the Internet could continue at some length. It is assumed, however, that other articles in this volume will provide greater detail on available sites and services. The above examples are meant to show that the Internet is beginning to have substance as a career planning and job searching resource; however, it is a long way from being a primary source. At this time, specific job and career information sites on the Internet supplement other traditional resources. There are many issues to be resolved before it will be a primary resource. For example, given the instability of Internet resources in general, it would come as no suprise to find that by the time this article is in print, a number of the sites mentioned may no longer be available at the address given. On the other hand, some of the sites will not only stablize, but also will increase in coverage. In addition, many new career/job sites will be added. This will require librarians and others to regularly monitor, or "surf," the Net for these additions, as well as keep up with professional readings and listserv messages for mention of new sites. Then it's a matter of incorporating these into one's repertoire of resources to turn to for career and job information.

INSTRUCTION:
BARRIERS AND BENEFITS

Until recently, library instruction focused on the physical building and the library collection. But Ranganathan's fifth Law of Library Science, "The library is a growing organism," is truer than ever. In the networked environment, the library is viewed as a gateway to worldwide information; therefore, once trained, librarians must participate in patron instruction. Given the rate of change and increased growth of electronic information, it seems to be such that planning for continual training and retraining is a required course of action (Notsinger, 1994).

Librarians and career and job professionals are developing new roles to play in the world of electronic information. Tim Lynch (1994) presented six key roles: maintainer (assist with maintenance and support), interpreter, trainer, enabler, liaison, and advisor, and to this list can be added advocator, organizer, builder, leader, and evaluator. As society begins to assimilate the Internet, resource evaluation will be essential. A lot of information is traveling on the Internet, but no one person or institution is saying what it should mean, and no one is vouching for it or evaluating it. Much of it is just dross; for example, someone putting out their science fiction novel that no one else would buy (Stoll, 1995).

A key role for librarians at this time is that of trainer. The Internet requires instruction. However, instruction is complicated by issues of access equity and information literacy. Remember, a library card is free, but getting and staying connected can be costly. Secondly, even though access is being gained to the Net through the use of graphical interfaces with sound capabilities, the Internet is strongly text driven. If a patron can't read, he or she will find it difficult to surf the Net. Even when access is assured, one writer noted, "There is an educational disconnect between the rapidly developing communications technologies and information resources available to the public, and the public's ability to use these resources" (McClure, 1994). Librarians and career and job professionals are in a primary position to help fill these voids, either by directing a patron's use of the Internet, or by utilizing the Net on behalf of the patron.

The lines that used to distinguish the computer center from the library are now blurred. In short, BI is no longer the domain of libraries, but is being shared with systems personnel. Internet training puts a whole new spin on bibliographic instruction by crossing over into a technical arena, and this requires knowing something about the hardware, software, key strokes, and commands. Until this technical knowledge is established, issues of content cannot be presented. Though it may seem to be an overworked message, training should be a collaborative effort between librarians and computer center and systems personnel. After all, information technology as required by the Internet was not part of the education most librarians received in library school. At the same time, patron service and information management and evaluation were not part of the education most systems personnel received in their education. Librarians and systems people both bring a background to the Internet, and both stand to learn a great deal about the Internet from each other.

CONCLUSION

Skills in accessing electronic information will be crucial to success in the coming decade, especially for librarians, career planning and job search professionals. There is a great need to explore how the Internet will assist career planning and employment needs. "Experimentation and risk taking need to be encouraged, and innovation is to be required to try out new paradigms of service" (Mardikian, 1995). Those associated with libraries are in a prime position to make the transition, incorporate Internet resources into the service structure, and provide instruction to others in how it can benefit them. Those who do assimilate the Internet will provide better service, and those who don't will be left behind.

REFERENCES

Booker, Ellis (1994). Job Seekers Scan Electronic Horizon. *Computerworld*, 28 (40): 1, 133.

Kilian, Crawford (1994). Why Teachers Fear the Internet. *Internet World*, 5 (8): 86-87.

Lynch, Tim (1994). The Many Roles of an Information Technology Section. *Library Hi Tech* 12 (3): 38-43.

Mardifian, Jackie and Martin Kesselman (1995). Beyond the Desk: Enhanced Reference Staffing for the Electronic Library. *Reference Services Review*, 23 (1): 21-28.

McClure, Charles R. (1994). Network Literacy: A Role for Libraries. *Information Technology and Libraries* 13 (2): 115-126.

Nofsinger, Mary M. and Allan W. Bosch (1994). Roles of the Head of Reference: From the 1990s to the 21st Century. *The Reference Librarian* 43, pgs. 87-99.

Peck, S. Hughes (1994). Teacher Training is the Key. *Byte* 19 (11): 366.

Stoll, Clifford (1995). *Silicon Snake Oil: Second Thoughts on the Information Highway*. New York: Doubleday.

II. THE RESOURCES

A Basic Guide to Job Search Resources on the Internet

Vivian Catherine Jones

SUMMARY. Job searching is often a frustrating experience, due in part to the lack of an organized and convenient method to gather information on careers, career development and job leads. The Internet is quickly becoming an efficient means for gaining access to all of these resources. This paper lists and describes several relatively stable Internet sites containing information and job postings. In addition, monitoring Usenet newsgroups and listservs to look for position announcements is also discussed. Finally, several comprehensive guides to job searching on the Internet are cited and discussed. *[Article copies available from The Haworth Document Delivery Service: 1-800-342-9678. E-mail address: getinfo@haworth.com]*

INTRODUCTION

Job searching, often a frustrating and demoralizing experience, is a process that the average American will go through eight times in

Vivian Catherine Jones is Research Assistant, Congressional Research Service, Economics Division, Library of Congress, Washington, D.C.

[Haworth co-indexing entry note]: "A Basic Guide to Job Search Resources on the Internet." Jones, Vivian Catherine. Co-published simultaneously in *The Reference Librarian* (The Haworth Press, Inc.) No. 55, 1996, pp. 19-29; and: *Career Planning and Job Searching in the Information Age* (ed: Elizabeth A. Lorenzen) The Haworth Press, Inc., 1996, pp. 19-29. Single or multiple copies of this article are available from The Haworth Document Delivery Service [1-800-342-9678, 9:00 a.m. - 5:00 p.m. (EST). E-mail address: getinfo@haworth.com].

his or her lifetime. Richard Nelson Bolles attributes much of the difficulty to what he calls the "outdated, outmoded and Neanderthal job-hunting apparatus"[1] one must use to find a job in this country. One major problem has been with gaining information on career development ideas, job searching techniques and job leads in an organized and orderly manner. That situation is on its way to being rectified due to a rapidly expanding number of Internet sites offering anything from practical information on interviewing techniques to a forecast of what occupations and the workplace will look like in the year 2005. Government agencies and corporations are increasingly providing job leads on the Internet and, while doing so, are providing links to valuable sources of career development information–rapidly making the Internet a very effective electronic library for the job-hunter.

This paper "visits" several gopher, telnet and World Wide Web sites[2] on the Internet that provide career development information, resume database services and electronic job postings. Finally, Internet guides dealing with electronic resources for job-hunting will be cited. The Uniform Resource Locator (URL, or "Internet address") for each site is cited in the appendix at the end of this volume, and this article will give descriptions of the information available within these resources. The URLs for the Internet sites were current at the date of this writing, but may be subject to change.

CHARTING THE COURSE:
CAREER DEVELOPMENT RESOURCES

Before beginning the job hunt, it is helpful to take stock of one's abilities and career goals, to look at employment trends in the field one is considering, and even to consider going into business for oneself. One career development reference tool is the Department of Labor's annual publication, the *Occupational Outlook Handbook*. The University of Missouri-St. Louis has made this invaluable resource available on its gopher site. This reference work contains information on 250 occupations in detail and information on 77 other jobs. Ninety-four percent of all occupations in the United States are explained in a structured and organized format. The type and nature of work, advancement possibilities, earnings and future job outlook are discussed for each profession or trade. In addition, sources of information about career preparation such as resume writing and interviewing are given. Career opportunities and occupations of the future are also discussed, outlining trends in U.S. industry and employment through the year 2005.[3]

The International Trade Administration of the Department of Commerce also publishes an annual document, the *Industrial Outlook Handbook,* also available in full text at the same gopher site. This reference work forecasts increases and declines in 200 manufacturing and service industries in the United States. Forecasts in the 1994 edition are based largely on economic and trade data in the third quarter of 1993 and concurrent economic projections. The recent history and trends in each of the industries is also discussed.[4]

The *1993 State Industry Profiles,* issued by the Small Business Administration provide a wealth of small business information in each of the fifty states. This information is extremely useful for the budding entrepreneur as he or she begins to think of business locations, possible competition, and setting up a business plan.[5] The same agency also provides the *1993 U.S. Industry Profiles* which documents current practices, employment trends, problems and successes in United States industry and makes educated assumptions regarding the future of each industry mentioned.[6]

Career development resources have also been made available at a number of commercial and "private" Internet sites. The *Online Career Center,* for example, gives bibliographic and price information on several publications regarding the electronic job hunt. Information on recruiters and employment agencies is also available, as is a source regarding current U.S. immigration law.

A Compendium of Women's Resources, developed by Jessie Stickgold-Sarah, provides useful links to information on women in computer science, medicine and health care, academia and other occupations. Especially helpful are links to a "Directory of Women's Professional Organizations" and to a bibliography on women in science, health and technology.

These are a few major resources on career development and entrepreneurship available on the Internet. For more information on these sites, refer to the three Internet guides on the topic mentioned at the end of this paper.

RESUME DATABASE SERVICES

The *Online Career Center,* available to both World Wide Web and gopher users, is a non-profit cooperative of employers dedicated to developing and implementing an electronic employment, advertising and communications system for human resource management.[7] Cost for system maintenance is borne by employers who contribute a one-time entrance fee to the cooperative and advertise positions in the employment listings at the site. Resumes in ASCII format can be posted by e-mail to occ-resumes@iquest.net. The subject line of the e-mail message will become the resume title when it is posted, therefore it is best to use a "catchy" or informative self-description so that a prospective employer will notice it. The resume will stay on the system for 90 days and may be updated at any time by e-mailing a newer version (the original will disappear). Job seekers without Internet access may mail a typed copy of their resume (up to three pages of text, including cover letter) to Online Resume Service, 1713 Hemlock Lane, Plainfield, IN 46168 with a $10.00 service charge. The resume will be typed on the database and will stay in the system for six months.

Resumes posted on the Online Career Center are not confidential, meaning that anyone may browse the resumes posted on the database. This provides a valuable career development resource for those who are interested in gathering ideas for their own resumes and in finding out how their talents and experience compare with other job searchers in their field. However, the non-confidential status may present a problem for applicants who may not want to make it known that they are job-hunting or for other reasons wish to keep their resumes private.

The *HEART System,* or "On-line Interactive Recruitment Network"[R] is also free to job seekers. It is possible to post a resume, respond to a particular position, communicate with a recruiter, and conduct an on-line interview in real time on the same network. At this time, resumes may only be posted by dialing in to the system and by uploading them in ASCII format using transfer protocols such Xmodem and Zmodem (an ftp site is available for posting resumes to specific employers). The dial-in number is (415) 903-5830 (2400 baud); (415) 903-7815 (9600/14400 baud). Communications software should be set to accommodate 8 data bits, No parity, 1 stop bit, ANSI/VT100 terminal emulation. It is also possible via telnet to fill out a detailed personal profile questionnaire that is used by the system to create a resume. Resumes stored on the system are completely confidential. The job seeker responds to a specific job posting on the system by posting his or her resume directly to the employer or recruiter.[8]

The *Direct Marketing World Jobs Center* is a new and more informal site on which job seekers may post resumes or brief personal profiles. Resumes must be in ASCII format to be mailed to the Center.

JOB LISTINGS ON THE INTERNET

Both HEART and the Online Career Center make an effort to have nationwide listings in a wide variety of fields. At the date of this writing, Online Career Center postings are heavily high-tech oriented and the HEART system has postings for only a limited number of jobs. However, there are many other databases operated by professional associations, academic institutions, and commercial organizations that offer a wide variety of job postings.

Many universities and professional organizations post electronic job listings. Many of these sites provide information on jobs available only within the specific association or academic community; however, some sites also provide gateways to related job information nationwide.

Two sites that post listings for college administrators, academics and other professionals with credentials and/or experience in higher education are *Academe this Week* and *Academic Position Network. Academe this Week,* the *Chronicle of Higher Education*'s gopher site, provides a searchable version of all job postings included in the weekly publication. Searches can be made by area of the country, by *Academe's* listing of job titles, or by entering a keyword of one's own choosing. The *Academic Position Network* also posts position announcements for professionals in higher education as well as providing information on post-doctoral positions, graduate fellowships and assistantships. Postings are organized by country, state, and institution and searching with Boolean operators is allowed.

ARTJOB, a service of the Western States Arts Federation, posts current national and international job listings in all areas of the arts. Positions at non-profit arts agencies, presenting organizations, producing organizations and academic institutions are well represented, as are opportunities for artistic performance. Related information on grants, competitions, conferences and internships is also posted.

Job seekers in business-related professions can refer to Stanford University's *Yahoo List*. The Yahoo List provides links to many of the Internet resources listed in this article, as well as to many other sites offering employment for those in business and management. Those interested in management or broadcasting careers in public radio and television can refer to the Corporation for Public Broadcasting's *Jobline* available through the Yahoo List. The *Direct Marketing World Jobs Center*, mentioned above (also in the Yahoo List), contains a good selection of both technical and non-technical (mostly sales) positions. *Medsearch America* lists administrative and health care positions posted by pharmaceutical companies, sports medicine clinics, cancer treatment centers, biotech firms, HMOs, etc. Those seeking entry-level, middle-level and senior positions in business and management have access to hundreds of current postings through the Yahoo List and other Internet sites.

Jobs for computer specialists and software engineers are abundantly represented in the Online Career Center's job listings (mentioned above) as well as at *CareerMosaic* and *The Monster Board*. CareerMosaic is run by Bernard Hodes Advertising and charges the companies listing jobs for their participation. Information about the corporations is also posted—including company profiles and information about work sites and employee benefits. The Monster Board includes over 300 positions from more than fifty companies. Most of the jobs listed at these sites are in the field of computing but marketing, communications and other positions also appear in smaller numbers.[9]

Positions in the federal government are posted at several Internet locations. The most reliable, stable and searchable site is the Office of Personnel Management's *FJOB*. Job files may be searched or browsed by series (select "help" for a complete listing of series titles and numbers) or job title or may be displayed by state. *Fedworld,* a U.S. government Internet server operated by the National Technological Information Service (NTIS), is another very reliable site. The electronic job files are long and the searching ability is rudimentary at this point; however, files can be read/ scrolled through on-line, downloaded using tranfer protocols such as ASCII, Zmodem or Kermit if the searcher dials into the system, or retrieved from the ftp site in the "jobs" subdirectory. The Fedworld job files are updated daily, Tuesday through Saturday, normally by 8 a.m. EST, and are collected from the OPM database mentioned above.

A database listing job postings specifically for librarians is maintained by the Graduate School of Library and Information Science at the University of Illinois at Urbana-Champaign. Listings may be searched by level of experience, area of librarianship desired, date of posting and geographic location. Updates to the list are made frequently and compiled from job listings sent directly to the school.

Postings for research scientists, mathematicians and economists are represented in three databases, respectively. *Academic Physician and Scientist (APS)* lists over 400 positions in academic medicine from 126 affiliated medical schools and teaching hospitals. Administrative positions, positions in basic science, clinical science postings and opportunities with the Food and Drug Administration are included.[7] Jobs for mathematicians with advanced degrees are listed by the *American Mathematical Society.* The vast majority of these positions are in academe. Entries to the list are standardized so that although positions are not in a searchable format, the listings are fairly easy to scan.[8] *Job Opportunities for Economists (JOE)* is a large collection of job postings for economists published by the American Economic Association. Most of the positions are academic listings which require a doctoral degree; however, there are a number of listings at business and non-profit organizations with less stringent requirements.

LISTSERVS AND USENET NEWSGROUPS

Listservs are subject-oriented e-mail discussion lists that are generally scholarly in nature and are moderated by one or more "list-owners" or "sysops" who loosely monitor discussions and forward messages on to list participants. Many listservs are associated with professions in which participants in the e-mail list group post position announcements related to the focus of the list, but some listservs are more narrowly focused and include only job postings (*SLAJOB*, the Special Libraries Association job list, is a good example of the latter).

Diane Kovacs has compiled a fairly comprehensive "list of listservs" that is available through North Carolina State University's *"Library Without Walls."* The list may either be browsed or searched and is organized according to broad disciplines. A table of contents and index are also attached to the list. E-mail addresses, moderators' names, and directions for subscribing to the listserv are given.

To sign on to a listserv, the user sends an e-mail message to the address given for the desired listserv. The subject line of the message should remain blank. The body of the message should contain the command "SUBSCRIBE name of list (ie. libref-l@kentvm.edu) [your] firstname [and] lastname." The subscriber automatically receives two e-mail messages from the system welcoming him or her to the listserv and informing the new user of procedures and commands to use when posting messages, signing off the list, etc. These messages should be saved for future reference.[10]

Usenet newsgroups, some of which are generally more informal, are unmoderated subject-oriented discussion groups. Michigan State University is one gopher site at which usenet messages can be read, although a Usenet software package like "Trumpet" is a much more satisfactory method by which to participate in a group. There are numerous Usenet newsgroups related to job-hunting, including *alt.jobs, misc.jobs.wanted* and *misc.jobs.offered*. Some newsgroups are local in nature, but many are accessible worldwide. For a listing of Usenet newsgroups involving job searching and career development, see Margaret Riley's Internet guide, *Employment Opportunities and Job Resources on the Internet.*

OTHER GOPHER AND WWW SITES

There are several World Wide Web and gopher sites that provide links to many of the Internet sites listed above. The best of these to date is a recently developed site *Job Search and Employment Opportunities: Best Bets from the Net,* which was developed and is currently maintained by Philip Ray and Bradley Taylor at the University of Michigan. The World Wide Web site provides hyperlinks to the Occupational Outlook Handbook and other U.S. government career development resources mentioned above, as well as several of the employment lists such as Online Career Center and CareerMosaic. This site is a "best bet" in itself as it provides links to some of the largest job databases and most stable job-seeking sites.

RiceInfo, Rice University in Texas' Campus Wide Information Service provides links to over 70 sites offering job and employment listings, including some links to major Usenet newsgroups (unfortunately these are not accessible to people searching from off-campus due to restrictions). Several links to colleges and universities nationwide are included, enabling the searcher to look for positions posted specific to those institutions as well as to browse listings in their respective career development offices.

LCMarvel offers current information on positions available at the Library of Congress and links to an expanding list of career and employment resources. Especially notable at this site is a general description of salaries and employment benefits provided to Federal employees. Stanford University's *Yahoo List,* mentioned above, provides links to many of the Internet resources listed in this article as well as to a wide array of job postings and career development information sites.

INTERNET GUIDES

Three regularly updated guides to job searching on the Internet are available on the Internet for reading and/or downloading. John Fenner has produced *Finding Library Jobs and Library Employment: Navigating the Electronic Web,* a useful guide that provides information on finding employment specifically in the field of librarianship. Another valuable guide is *Employment Opportunites and Job Resources on the Internet* by Margaret Riley of Worcester Polytechnic Institute. Ray and Taylor have also written a gopher (text) version of *Job Searching and Employment: Bets Bets from the*

Net, summarizing the resources available at their World Wide Web site by the same name. All three of these guides, along with numerous other subject-oriented Internet guides, are available in the virtual "stacks" of the University of Michigan.

CONCLUSION

There is a rapidly expanding array of information on career development and employment opportunities available on the Internet. This paper has provided descriptions of many resources available (with addresses available in the appendix of this volume) in the areas of career development, resume database services, and newsgroups and listservs containing job opportunites in a number of career fields. Internet guides providing a more in-depth look at employment resources on the net have also been cited. The expanding use of the Internet by many companies and professional associations for their recruitment activities has already added yet another dimension to the job searches of the many people seeking employment in the confusing maze that is the U.S. job market.

REFERENCES

1. Bolles, Richard Nelson, *The 1994 What Color is Your Parachute*, Berkeley, CA, 1994

2. See "Getting Started on the Net" by Karen Diaz (*The Reference Librarian*, No. 41/42, pp. 3-24) for a basic discussion of the Internet and related terminology.

3. U.S. Department of Commerce, Bureau of Labor Statistics. *Occupational Outlook Handbook 1994-1995*. Washington, DC: U.S. Government Printing Office. Electronic version made available by the libraries of the University of Missouri-St. Louis.

4. U.S. Department of Commerce, International Trade Administration. *Occupational Outlook Handbook, 1994 edition*, Washington, DC: U.S. Government Printing Office. Made available in electronic format by the libraries of the University of Missouri-St. Louis.

5. U.S. Small Business Administration. *1993 State Industry Profiles*. From the National Economic, Social and Environmental Data Bank. Made available on the Internet by the libraries of the University of Missouri-St. Louis.

6. U.S. Small Business Administration. *1993 U.S. Industry Profiles*. From the National Economic, Social and Environmental Data Bank. Made available on the Internet by the libraries of the University of Missouri-St. Louis.

7. Online Career Center, "Frequently Asked Questions."

8. The HEART System Online Interactive Recruitment Network[R] Information Center, "System Features," "About Us," and "Uploading a Resume."

9. The Monster Board, "Freqently Asked Questions."

10. Riley, Margaret, *Employment Opportunties and Job Resources on the Internet* (URL: http://www.jobtrack.com/jobguide).

The Internet Job Search:
Strategies for Locating Online Resources

Margaret F. Riley

SUMMARY. To many users, the Internet is an unfriendly and unusable network of computers, but for the job hunter, it contains a multitude of important information resources. Position listings, resume-writing assistance, company profiles, and other relevant pieces of information are available to the user who can locate them. This article outlines concepts and search strategies which can be used to find this information utilizing a variety of Internet tools and resources. *[Article copies available from The Haworth Document Delivery Service: 1-800-342-9678. E-mail address: getinfo@haworth.com]*

INTRODUCTION

Many ways exist to find information on the Internet, but locating and retrieving this information requires a familiarity with several Internet information networks and their accompanying software programs or "tools." The various Internet information networks—Usenet newsgroups, telnet sites, gopher and World Wide Web serv-

Margaret F. Riley is Circulation and Computer Resources Librarian, Worcester Polytechnic Institute, George C. Gordon Library, 100 Institute Road, Worcester, MA 01609. Email: mfriley@wpi.edu

The author thanks all those who gave her great advice and comments for this article.

[Haworth co-indexing entry note]: "The Internet Job Search: Strategies for Locating Online Resources." Riley, Margaret F. Co-published simultaneously in *The Reference Librarian* (The Haworth Press, Inc.) No. 55, 1996, pp. 31-41; and: *Career Planning and Job Searching in the Information Age* (ed: Elizabeth A. Lorenzen) The Haworth Press, Inc., 1996, pp. 31-41. Single or multiple copies of this article are available from The Haworth Document Delivery Service [1-800-342-9678, 9:00 a.m. - 5:00 p.m. (EST) E-mail address: getinfo@haworth.com].

ers, and mailing lists and electronic publications—all carry information and listings relevant to the job hunt and accessible to the job hunter. The basic strategy for locating information on the Internet does not appear difficult; first, determine where to look for the information desired, then decide the best way to retrieve it. Job hunters can decide which Internet networks and resources are more likely to provide the information desired based on some general characteristics for each network and its resources and then select the best method for retrieving the information. This article will discuss the various information networks, outline general characteristics of each network and its resources relative to the job hunt, and present methods for finding these resources.

Given the complexity of the Internet, why should the job hunter want to incorporate this rapidly expanding network of networks into an already demanding search for employment? The growth of available information resources is one reason. Online listings of employment opportunities along with information about companies and their products are becoming more accessible. Reports on salaries in various professions, employment statistics, and other topics important to the job hunter are also available. The ability to use the resources and services of the Internet at any time of the day, night, or weekend is another reason. The search for job listings and the application for employment using electronic mail can take place at any time of the day or night. The geographic reach of the Internet is a third reason. For example, the job hunter can be living in Boston but searching in San Francisco or Paris since listings for these areas can be accessed locally. Finally, locating and responding to job listings found on the Internet demonstrates to a potential employer a skill which may set the job hunter apart from other applicants for the same position, namely familiarity with the Internet and the ability to navigate its complex structure.

USENET NEWSGROUPS

Overview

The newsgroups comprising the Usenet are a major resource for job listings, resume postings, and discussion groups on job hunting.

Most job listings on the Usenet are posted by companies or corporate recruiters as opposed to academic, research, or government recruiters. *Bionet.jobs.** and *sci.research.careers* are notable exceptions to this general rule. The information carried on this network is very current, fast-paced, and constantly changing. Job hunters who decide to incorporate Usenet newsgroups into their search strategy should check the newsgroups daily for new listings and announcements, and they should be prepared to respond quickly to submit resumes and letters.

Usenet newsgroups can be international in coverage (*misc.jobs.**), local to a geographic area (*ba.jobs.*,* the San Francisco Bay area) or specific to one organization (*umn.*,* the newsgroups of the University of Minnesota). Job hunters who are interested in relocating to another geographic area can conduct a search locally for positions anywhere in the U.S. or abroad by using those newsgroups specific to his/her preferred final location.

Searching for Usenet Newsgroups

The varied structures, or "hierarchies," of the Usenet are a challenge to monitor for job listings and related information. While certain hierarchies and newsgroups remain constant, others come and go on an almost daily basis. The major difficulty lies in finding the various groups as they become available and providing access to them. If a site carries Usenet newsgroups, it is possible that many relevant groups are already available but the job hunter is not "subscribed" to them, meaning they are not displayed when reading news. There are commands in the newsreader programs (rn, trn, tin, etc.) which will list these unsubscribed newsgroups. The job hunter can then add these to the newsgroup list using the program's "subscribe" command.

The system administrator who monitors the news feed locally determines which groups carried by the selected news feed service will be readable at each site. Announcements of new newsgroups carried by this service will also go to this person. It is important to involve him/her in the search for newsgroups carrying job listings and other relevant information and discussions. *Employment Opportunities and Job Resources on the Internet,* a public guide to free job listings and related resources, lists about 100 job-related newsgroups available through Usenet. This list could be used as a bench-mark for checking local newsgroup availability. Enlist the participation of the system administrator in looking for the *.jobs* and other useful groups and request that they be carried locally. If the system administrator does not want to provide access to all of these, or if the news feed service does not carry the local or organizational hierarchies, the *misc.jobs.** groups and some of the more academic groups such as *bionet.jobs.** and *sci.research.careers* should satisfy most users. Many local groups cross-post to these worldwide groups, so a large percentage of the job listings on the Usenet can be accessed through these few here.

More Resources for Locating Newsgroup Information

Some newsgroups are archived at various gopher sites around the Internet. A *Veronica* search using the name of these groups will reveal their locations to you. Various listings of newsgroups are posted to the *news.lists* newsgroup, and these can also be down-loaded via anonymous ftp and searched using any word processing program. Two of the more important lists to use in locating job-related groups are the *List of All Active Newsgroups* which covers the more mainstream hierarchies, and the *List of All Usenet Newsgroups* which includes many lesser-known local and organizational hierarchies.

MAILING LISTS AND ELECTRONIC NEWSLETTERS

Overview

Mailing lists cover a broad variety of topics in various disciplines. Occasional job announcements are carried on these lists, usually in advance of a similar announcement in print resources. The poster of these jobs is addressing a specific group of people with certain professional and/or personal interests and expertise. Most posted positions are in academic or research-related institutions and require a graduate or post-graduate degree; however, an occasional corporate position will be posted. Hundreds of mailing lists are available for many disciplines and interests, making these an important resource, especially for the higher-level job seeker. Mailing lists are also forming for the express purpose of carrying job announcements. For example, *FrogJobs* was created to carry announcements of scientific positions in France. Since these resources operate through electronic mail, the job hunter will be notified when new announcements and listings are sent to subscribers. The mail file should be checked daily for any new messages. While the response to a posted position need not be instantaneous, it should not be delayed.

Electronic journals and newsletters used to be similar to the mailing lists in their coverage of research topics, but now hundreds of commercial and popular journals can be received via the Internet for no cost and more are available for a fee. Many of these carry job announcements like their print companions. The publication's intended audience (academic, corporate, or general audience) will determine the type of job listings included. Careful consideration of the publication's description and examination of a few issues may be needed to ensure relevance to the job hunter. As with fee-based print journals and newsletters, the job hunter should request a sample copy before purchasing a subscription. A check of the job hunter's mail file will alert him/her to the arrival of new announcements.

Searching for Mailing Lists and Other Electronic Print Resources

The best resource for information about the academic mailing lists and electronic journals is *The Directory of Electronic Newsletters, Journals, and Academic Discussion Lists* published by the Association of Research Libraries. The print version is updated annually, but this information is also available on the *ARL gopher*. In addition, *NewList* and *NewJour-L* are two mailing lists created to announce new mailing lists and electronic journals. Job hunters who want to take this search beyond the more academic topics can also consult the Liszt of Email Discussion Lists, which includes not only mailing lists but a searchable list of over 15,000 Usenet newsgroups.

More Resources for Locating Mailing List Information

A single service to monitor for announcements of all types of new Internet resources including mailing lists and electronic journals is the *Net-Happenings* mailing list. The operators of this list survey several Internet services used to announce new information resources and services. They then post the most important information in one location, eliminating the need for the job hunter to monitor several separate resources. The postings from this list are archived online with a full-text index for search and retrieval of information.

The Clearinghouse for Subject-Oriented Internet Resource Guides is another valuable resource for all types of Internet information. This service housed at the University of Michigan School of Information and Library Studies inlcudes over 160 guides covering topics from art history to women's studies, each list being an annotated bibliography of the Internet resources which carry information on the given subject; newsgroups, telnet sites, gopher and web sites, mailing lists, and any other Internet resource the authors find to be relevant are included. The Clearinghouse features a single full-text index encompassing all of the guides housed here, and a search returns a menu of those guides which contain your keyword(s).

TELNET SITES

Overview

The telnet sites which carry job listings and other career resources are often the most difficult to locate because no list or index to these sites exists. Corporate listings are available through recruiters such as *H.E.A.R.T.,* Career Connections's online employment network. A number of state and federal government agencies also list their positions at various sites, and some of the professional societies are offering telnet access to job listings sent to them by academic and other institutions. These listings may change weekly, and many sites have a specific day of the week or month when new listings are added. Once relevant sites have been located, the job hunter will want to check these listings when new postings are due or a minimum of once a week.

Searching for Telnet Resources

Most telnet resources are discovered by scanning various directories of Internet information, by monitoring services which announce new Internet resources, and by word of mouth. A more standardized way to locate these resources is by using the *Hytelnet* program and by monitoring the *Hytel-L* mailing list. While library catalogs dominate Hytelnet, connections and information on several other resources are also included, such as the growing number of freenets located around the United States and Canada. Many of these services carry local and government job listings for their region and offer other career-related information.

More Resources for Locating Telnet Information

After Hytelnet and the Hytel-L mailing list, the *Net-Happenings* mailing list and the *Clearinghouse* server are the best locations to search for telnet-accessible resources. Any announcement or listing of an organization or network accessible through telnet should be checked for job listings.

GOPHER

Overview

While the growth rate of the Gopher network has slowed recently, it has not stopped. This network still carries the majority of the academic sites both in the U.S. and internationally, and the U.S. Federal Government still has a commanding presence here. Professional societies representing several disciplines maintain gopher sites and collect job listings which are accessible to all Internet users. Many colleges and universities include their open positions on their gopher servers. Persons searching for positions in academe or related research fields as well as for work in the U.S. Federal Government are best directed to this network of information resources.

In addition to the academic and government services, some corporate recruiters have set up gopher sites offering access to the available job listings of their various subscribers and recruiting employees on the Internet. Many online recruiters offer resume banks into which a resume can be placed at no cost to the job hunter. These files are then made available to corporate recruiters for a fee. *The Online Career Center* is one such site. They offer not only job listings in all fields and a resume bank, but also include several additional files with job-hunting tips and other career-related resources. Job listings and information resources on gophers are generally not changed on a daily basis. Weekly or semiweekly checks of relevant sites should be sufficient.

Searching for Gopher Resources

The *Veronica* index is the major resource for finding information in gopher sites, but it can be problematic. The Veronica index is so large that the resulting search list can be overwhelming even to a more experienced user. The information retrieved must be carefully sorted to find the most useful or relevant listings, a somewhat time-consuming process. Before making a first attempt at a search, the job hunter should read the file *"How to Compose Veronica Queries"* found on the main menu. This is worth downloading or printing to have on hand for a quick reference to the commands and search parameters available. Keep these few basic guidelines in mind to help limit the amount of information retrieved in a single search:

1. Use two words for the keyword search when possible, especially when searching general terms such as "employment" or "resume."
2. Tell the Veronica server to look for gopher information by type of entry. Files (-t0) and directories (-t1) are two entry types of most use to the job hunter.
3. Decide if the information sought is more likely to be in a directory or a file. A directory search means the keywords will be found at the top of a menu structure which will include more resources below it. Listings of employment opportunities are more likely to be found within directories while information on employment statistics and other similar reports are more often found in files.

4. Different search terms produce different results. Be prepared to use alternate keywords to find more information or otherwise alter the search results.

More Resources for Locating Gopher Information

While Veronica is the main index of gopher entries, it is frequently busy and users may have trouble connecting to any one of the servers. Some gopher sites have added multiple links to other resources in their menus, using a broad subject index to organize these links. Two of these sites are the *Gopher Jewels* at the University of Southern California and *RiceInfo* at Rice University. If Veronica is not available, try these other resources along with searching the *Net-Happenings* archive and the *Clearinghouse* resource guides.

WORLD WIDE WEB RESOURCES

Overview

The World Wide Web, or the Web as it is more commonly known, has seen a tremendous amount of growth recently, the most of any Internet information network. While much of this growth has been due to academic institutions establishing web servers, many new servers have been registered by commercial users. The fact that corporate America is establishing a formidable presence there is a benefit for those seeking employment. A job hunter researching a company should be able to locate some relevant information on that company's web server. In addition, many companies are including their currently available positions on their servers as one more means of recruiting the best employees they can find. Many academic servers also list available positions at their institutions. This dual presence by both corporate and academic organizations makes the Web is a good resource for persons searching in either area.

Several recruiting agencies are establishing servers on the Web, offering various services and information to the job junter. Most agencies include not only job listings and resume banks but also have information about the companies for whom they are recruiting along with other career-related resources. In keeping with the evolution of the online job hunt, some agencies permit the job hunter to apply for a position while viewing the listings by using Lynx, NCSA Mosaic, or any other forms-capable browser. *The Monster Board, CareerMosaic,* and *E-Span* are three recruiting agencies maintaining web servers, each agency offering a unique set of resources for the job hunter.

Along with the recruiters and organizations listing their own positions, several professional societies have web servers which include job listings. The *SPIE Online Employment Service* includes position announcements categorized by the degree required, Ph.D., M.S, or B.S. Membership in the society is not necessary for application to these positions. Collections of pointers to job listings and other relevant information also exist on many servers. *The Job Resource List at Texas A&M University* has a large collection of pointers to more job hunting resources.

The Web's hyperlinked environment permits information to be added to and updated quickly, some sites performing daily updates of their listings. Once the job hunter identifies primary locations for job listings, a daily check of these sites is necessary to stay informed. In addition, weekly or semiweekly checks for new services and resources is also important.

Searching for Web Resources

Finding information on the Web is still a difficult process. The number of resources accessed through this network is growing rapidly and new information and services are being added daily while others are deleted. Resources are constantly shifting and changing as better methods of presentation and arrangement are developed and new computers are brought online to handle the demand for access. The mechanism for arranging this material into useful or meaningful categories for ease of access is far behind the development of the network. Various types of indexing and searching tools are being developed, and some sites are beginning to arrange links to web resources by subject as was done with the gopher sites. These "virtual libraries" along with the various indexing/searching tools are the best means to find information carried on the Web. Like on gopher, the Web's "virtual libraries" maintain links to information files, directories, and other services with relevant information on a given topic. Some have added a search mechanism to permit a keyword search over all links included in the "library." The *Virtual Library (CERN)* is one such service, and the *NCSA Meta-Index* is a second helpful starting point.

The various Web indexing/searching tools all have different strengths and weaknesses, and they all gather and index information differently. The job hunter will have to try these various tools and decide which are the most productive and user-friendly for his/her purposes. The *Galaxy* server offers a friendly search program, and it maintains links to several other virtual libraries, indexers, and other Internet information search tools. It automatically limits the search results to a manageable number of listings, but this default limit can be easily reset or the search repeated with new parameters. Another good indexer is the *WWW Worm* created by Oliver McBryan. Information on companies and their products can be easily located by using the "Search Titles of citing documents" and "Search Names of citing documents" options.

CONCLUSION

The Internet is an overwhelming and disorganized network of information resources, but there is useful information out there for the job hunter. Job listings are being added to the Internet by both academic institutions and companies, information about employers is being made accessible, and other useful information relevant to the job hunt is available. Job hunters can find this information by following several basic strategies. First of all, they must know the general characteristics of the various Internet networks to determine location of resources. They must then proceed to both learn and implement the methods suggested to locate and retrieve the information. Finally, they must be constantly monitoring the Internet for new listings and information. Utilizing these methods in order to search the Internet for employment opporunities and other relevant information should put the job hunter in a much more competitive position for consideration by prospective employers.

Job Searching on the World Wide Web

Ann O'Bryan Cockerham

SUMMARY. The Internet is being increasingly used both by job seekers and companies as a resource for employment opportunities and recruiting. Job listings, career development "centers," and company information are available on every internet tool: listservs, newsgroups, gophers, telnet sites, and the World Wide Web. This article will explore the capabilities of the Web as a tool for finding employment and developing a career. *[Article copies available from The Haworth Document Delivery Service: 1-800-342-9678. E-mail address: getinfo@haworth.com]*

INTRODUCTION

The World Wide Web is the fastest growing area of the Internet. Its graphical user interface, multimedia support, hypertext capability, and the variety of web browsers available make it extremely popular with the growing number of individuals, companies, and institutions with Internet access. New Internet users are attracted to the Web because it is easy to use, it does not require a high level of technical knowledge, and it has been successfully marketed in the popular computer magazines. Further, web browsers include all of

---

Ann O'Bryan Cockerham is Electronic Information Services and Catalog Librarian, Indiana State University Library, Indiana State University, Terre Haute, IN 47809. Email: libcham@cml.indstate.edu

The author thanks Indiana State University for its support of the research and writing of this article.

[Haworth co-indexing entry note]: "Job Searching on the World Wide Web." Cockerham, Ann O'Bryan. Co-published simultaneously in *The Reference Librarian* (The Haworth Press, Inc.) No. 55, 1996, pp. 43-49; and: *Career Planning and Job Searching in the Information Age* (ed: Elizabeth A. Lorenzen) The Haworth Press, Inc., 1996, pp. 43-49. Single or multiple copies of this article are available from The Haworth Document Delivery Service [1-800-342-9678, 9:00 a.m. - 5:00 p.m. (EST). E-mail address: getinfo@haworth.com].

43

the other Internet tools, such as telnet and gopher, so the whole Internet is open to those who have access to a web browser.

Many companies and institutions discovering the Internet via the Web are developing web pages. The marketing power of the Web is readily apparent when one goes to the homepages of companies, universities, and other institutions. The Web offers rich possibilities for presenting a company or institution's image–through graphics, multimedia, and hypertext–to a world-wide audience at little cost. The presence on the Internet, especially the Web, of such entities is growing rapidly. Therefore, information about potential employers is now more available and accessible than ever before. The potential "audience" is growing as well. The Internet is rapidly becoming accessible to more people, both in this country and abroad.

There are many Internet tools that provide access to career related resources. However, the Web offers new possibilities for the online job seeker. This article will focus on strategies to use the Web's unique features in an Internet job search.

STRENGTHS OF THE WEB

Interactivity

One of the Web's advantages over other Internet utilities lies in its interactive capability. With the use of HTML forms and the mail functions of some browsers it is possible to respond online to job notices. In addition, the job seeker may register a resume with an online career service, such as JobWeb. Forms also make it possible to limit searches in a variety of ways. For example, Career Mosaic's Jobs. offered database uses a form in which one may specify job description, job title, company name, city, state or province, zip or postal code, country, and the number of hits.

Hypertext Capability

The Web's hypertext capability makes it a powerful navigating tool. Hot links take the user directly to related points of interest, making travel on the Internet fast and easy. Also, companies and institutions with web pages can use hot links to organize information and direct users to other files, documents, and locations. Individuals with personal homepages or HTML'd resumes can use links similarly to organize information and direct potential employers to relevant files. Hypertext therefore can be used as a marketing tool as well as a navigational tool.

Multimedia

The Web's multimedia capability opens up a wealth of design possibilities. Companies and institutions can use graphics, sound, and video in the design of homepages to enhance marketing, thereby enabling potential employees to see a more complete image of the company or institution than what only text can portray. Individuals can use the same tools similarly in resumes and personal homepages.

WORD-ORIENTED SEARCH ENGINES

There are currently several Web search engines that search the entire Internet, similar to Veronica searching of gophers. Known by such names as crawlers, worms, spiders, and ants, these tools search the Internet in a variety of ways. For example, some search the contents of documents, while others search only the titles of documents and the URL contents. Using any of these utilities one may retrieve job notices from professional listservs, gopher servers, web sites, and virtually any other place on the Internet where jobs are posted. In addition, the job seeker can use these tools to search for company information and any other career-related resources.

CAREER RESOURCES ON THE WEB

Online Career Centers

Among the growing number of companies taking advantage of the possibilities of the Web are recruiting and career services firms. There are currently many online career "centers" that offer a variety of services from assistance in resume writing to searchable databases of job listings.

One such center is the Online Career Center. It offers information on career management; employment events, such as conferences and fairs; career-related resources for women and minorities; professional associations; and other career-related topics. In addition, it includes databases of jobs and resumes that are searchable by keyword or by browsing the listings. Further, job seekers may enter resumes to the Online Career Center database by using the online form.

Another commercial service is Career Mosaic. In addition to the database described above, it includes information on co-op opportunities, entry-level positions, and internship programs for college students and recent graduates. Like JobWeb, it includes information on career planning and other related topics.

Other similar Web sites include Careers Online, which lists positions in Europe, Asia, and the U.S.; E-Span's Interactive Employment Network, which offers resume and interviewing tips; and the Monster Board, which invites resumes from job seekers. All of these sites have searchable databases of job listings.

College and University Career Centers

Colleges and universities are adding the World Wide Web to their collection of Internet utilities, developing web pages representing academic and administrative departments. Career centers, which typically track trends in business and industry, are developing web pages that provide career planning information, pointers to job listings, links to commercial online career centers, and other topics of interest to new job seekers. Unlike other university departments that may use web pages to disseminate departmental or internal information, career centers are also serving as gateways to external information sources. In addition to information on departmental programs and organizations, many college and university career centers point to other sites that offer career-related information. Further, these online career centers often include information on graduate and professional programs, internships, fellowships, entry-level positions, and other information related to career planning and development. Although some are geared specifically to local students, many contain useful information for any college student preparing for a job search. Leo Charette has collected a large number of academic career centers in the Catapult.

Career center information and resources have been organized on web pages in a variety of ways. For instance, Brandeis University's Hiatt Career Development Center home page includes these categories: "Getting Started," with four menu items on using the Internet in the job search and other basic tips; "Special Topics," which includes articles especially geared for graduate students, women and minorities, and entrepreneurs, as well as information on choosing a major and sources for fellowships and financial aid; "Direct Access to Search Engines and Searchable Indices," which point directly to job listings and employer information; and "Guides to Career Resources on the Net," which includes guides by Margaret Riley and Leo Charette. The University of Illinois at Urbana-Champaign's Career Planning and Professional Development page is organized into Job-Hunting Tools for Students, Comprehensive Job-Hunting Services, Lists of Vacancies, Foreign Help-Wanted Lists, and Graduate School. Indiana State University's Career Resources page has categories for Job Postings (subdivided into Education, Government, and Business and Industry listings); Guides (including the Riley guide and ISU's Career Information guide); Online Job Search Services (with pointers to such services as CareerMosaic and the Monster Board); Career Services from Other Colleges and Universities; the Occupational Outlook Handbook; Community Information; and Employer Information.

Webbed Classifieds

Another growing trend is evident as newspapers begin to make their classified ads available over the Internet. One good example is the Chicago Tribune, which has put its classified ads online in the Chicago Tribune Career Finder. This site contains information on job opportunities, company profiles, and feature articles, as well as the job listings in five technical categories from the most recent issue of the Tribune.

Two other newspapers with classified employment ads include the San Francisco Examiner and the San Jose Mercury Sun. Webbed classifieds may definitely be an area of future growth on the Internet.

Other Webbed Resources

Internet subject "catalogs" are another source for career-related information. There are several such subject guides, and their number will probably increase in time. Three sites with career listings are EINet Galaxy, Yahoo, and the Whole Internet Catalog. These subject catalogs provide a good starting point, both for the first time user and for the library developing its own home page of resources.

LIMITATIONS OF THE WEB

Although the Web is growing rapidly, there still seem to be few sources for non-technical job listings. At this writing, a large majority of the companies with web sites are computer-related companies. This will probably change as more academic and professional institutions enter the Web; but at this point the job listings in such fields as education, academia, the arts, and health care are limited. However, the Web is perhaps a more convenient tool for searching for the jobs that are listed in other Internet areas, such as gophers and listservs, than other search utilities. For example, using a word-oriented search utility, such as Lycos and the Web Crawler, one may search the entire Internet and retrieve hits from professional listservs, online publications, and gopher listings, as well as all of the webbed career center listings. Even though there will inevitably be some false hits, using the Web as a search tool is effective and easy.

CONCLUSION

As use of the World Wide Web becomes more widespread, and as more kinds of information are added to it, its importance as a library resource increases. Librarians that work at public service desks will increasingly be faced with questions on how to search the Web. In addition, the Internet will become the most logical and convenient source for information in a wider range of subject areas. Career librarians, as well as other reference librarians, will find it a rich source for business and career information.

Finally, the Internet is changing and growing at such a pace that it is nearly impossible to write about it in print without being out-dated. The Web is still so new that it probably is less stable than more "established" Internet tools. As with any Internet utility, the stability and reliability of the sources depend upon those that maintain the sites. In writing this article, the author has attempted to cite only those sources that appear stable. However, there probably will be a great deal of change between the time of writing and the time of publication of this article. Nevertheless, the strategies suggested for using the World Wide Web should still prove effective despite the inevitable change and growth of the Internet.

III. SERVICES TO SPECIAL GROUPS

Characteristics of Generation X
and Implications for Reference Services
and the Job Search

Catherine A. Lee

SUMMARY. Today's students, members of Generation X, are in many ways different from the baby boomers who, for the most part, now design and provide most of the services in academic libraries. Xers have a fundamentally different world view that is being heavily explored in marketing and demographic circles, but not so much in the library literature. Recognizing a few major cultural differences may help librarians to better meet the changing needs of today's students. *[Article copies available from The Haworth Document Delivery Service: 1-800-342-9678. E-mail address: getinfo@haworth.com]*

INTRODUCTION

"Generation X"–Almost every major cultural institution has set out to reach them, including Hollywood, NIKE, Taco Bell and the

---

Catherine A. Lee is Head Librarian, Penn State DuBois Campus, DuBois, PA 15801. Email: CAL@psulias.psu.edu

[Haworth co-indexing entry note]: "Characteristics of Generation X and Implications for Reference Services and the Job Search." Lee, Catherine A. Co-published simultaneously in *The Reference Librarian* (The Haworth Press, Inc.) No. 55, 1996, pp. 51-59; and: *Career Planning and Job Searching in the Information Age* (ed: Elizabeth A. Lorenzen) The Haworth Press, Inc., 1996, pp. 51-59. Single or multiple copies of this article are available from The Haworth Document Delivery Service [1-800-342-9678, 9:00 a.m. - 5:00 p.m. (EST). E-mail address: getinfo@haworth.com].

51

Clinton Campaign, yet libraries have done little to target and serve what is quickly becoming our primary market.

The name "Generation X" was first used by and about British Boomer punk rockers as the name of a punk rock band fronted by Billy Idol. It came into more popular use after the 1991 publication of Canadian novelist Douglas Coupland's youth cult classic, *Generation X: Tales for an Accelerated Culture*. Coupland, himself born in 1961, employed it to describe his age mates born between 1961 and 1964, a quasi-generation not fitting in emotionally with the boomers that preceded them or demographically with the baby busters that followed. Since then, the term has been loosely adopted to refer to those of us born between 1961 and 1981, and has graced the covers of such popular periodicals as *The New York Times Magazine, New Republic, The Atlantic, Business Week, Fortune, Newsweek,* and *U.S. News and World Report.*

The year 1991 also saw the publication of the nonfiction *Generations: The History of America's Future, 1584-2069* by William Strauss and Neil Howe. Strauss and Howe coined the term "13ers" to describe those born between 1961 and 1981, referring to the fact that this generation is the 13th, counting back to the peers of Ben Franklin, to know the American flag and the Constitution. advocating these generational dividing lines, Strauss and Howe argue that this post-boom generation is actually *bigger* than the baby boom, 79 million compared with 69 million boomers. That would mean, no matter what you call them–Xers, 13ers, Baby Busters, Twentysomethings, or Slackers–this generation will become the nation's largest voting block by 1998.

X FACTORS

Many in higher education have already noticed that something is different about the current generation of traditional-age college students. David Cannon (1991 & 1994), director of research for the London-based PRL Consulting and an authority on the behavior of this generation of young employees, posits the thesis that today's students–Generation X–are different from the baby boomers who, for the most part, now design and provide the majority of our services in academia. Through extensive focus group research, Cannon has identified eight representative "X" factors:

1. *A craving for stimulation.* Xers have grown up in an age of media sound bites and infotainment. They want variety. They're looking for work that stimulates, entertains, and is meaningful. Boring, routine, or monotonous jobs are the ultimate turn-off to Xers.
2. *Need for personal contact.* Xers are culturally independent yet demand personal attention and feedback . . . from supervisors, faculty, and other professionals such as librarians and career advisors.
3. *Preference for concrete, specific information.* This is the area in which librarians and Xers are most likely to clash or miscommunicate. Xers want an information service, providing accurate, up-to-the-minute information, preferably packaged in a concise, laser-printed format which they can take away with them to view at their convenience.
4. *A desire to learn leading-edge technology.* Xers are savvy enough to always be on the look-out for new skills which will add to their knowledge and their resumes. They are attracted to cutting-edge technology and to professionals with technology expertise. Xers also like jobs that keep them on the learning curve.
5. *Searching for traditional goals.* Once an Xer's career is on track, he or she will put great effort into their personal affairs, striving for a good marriage and home life. Forty percent of people in their 20s are children of divorce. They do not want to re-experience it as adults. Xers also refuse to be workaholics at the expense of quality time devoted to recreation and family.
6. *Looking for the good-looking job.* Xers would like work that is "sexy," unique, or worthwhile. Entry-level, service sector, McJobs are a major turn-off.
7. *Emotionally repressed.* Xers are pragmatic and realistic with exceptional coping skills. They may seem superficial because they tend to keep deep emotions to themselves, trusting few people. They're fascinated by the exaggerated emotions in

soap operas and shows such as "Thirtysomething," which went off the air just as the first wave of Xers reached the age of thirty.

8. *Keeping options open.* The single most recurring statement made by the students in Cannon's focus groups was, "I want to keep my options open." They are postponing any commitment such as marriage or full-time employment. They generally are taking longer to finish college. College completion rates, seven years after high school graduation, fell from 58% for the Boomer class of 1972 to 37% for the Xer class of 1980 (Strauss & Howe, 1991, p. 325). They are also going to graduate schools in record numbers. Between 1970 and the mid-1980s, the percentage of freshmen planning to pursue graduate or professional degrees remained fairly stable at 49%-50%. In 1990, it exceeded 60% (Dey, 1991, p. 11).

IMPLICATIONS FOR LIBRARIES AND LIBRARY SERVICES

Cannon's research sheds light on several characteristics of Generation X that directly impact on their career and job search interactions with academic libraries and librarians. Being aware of these characteristics and accepting Cannon's observation that "Xs are not crazy about libraries," how can we best serve this sometimes reluctant constituency? One major way is to rethink our notions on the "silver platter." Academic librarians cling to their role as teachers and often view reference transactions as golden opportunities for students to learn how to find information. When students ask for "the resume books," do we direct them to the online catalog and proceed to instruct them in the nuances of subject versus keyword searching? If an Xer comes looking for company information, do we point to Compact Disclosure, recommending several help sheets, the online tutorial, or the CD-ROM searching workshop the business librarian will be offering next week? Or, worse yet, would we suggest they browse through the business stacks; there's plenty of information located in the HDs through HGs? This sometimes inordinate emphasis on process establishes barriers between students and the information they seek.

There are still ample opportunities for us to teach Xers. Librarians can take advantage of the Xers' desire to learn leading-edge, marketable skills by offering hands-on Internet workshops on such topics as the electronic job search, business and company information, and government information sources. An entire workshop can be built around the topic of navigating the Online Career Center.

We could, moreover, take advantage of team teaching opportunities. Consider planning a pair of workshops in conjunction with the campus career development and placement office—they host a session on writing the resume and we show students how to upload it to the appropriate Internet sites. Additionally, we might host a series of workshops on the subject-specific databases in the library and invite faculty, alumni, and local business and professional people to participate. Students can use this as a networking opportunity in addition to learning the mechanics and the value of locating information in their chosen field. We could solicit faculty support by asking program leaders or department heads to recommend local guests and refer students. These sessions could be held as stand-alone workshops or in conjunction with other activities, such as job fairs or homecoming, which generally attract alumni and professionals to the campus.

Adopting an "information provider" role does not mean sacrificing our teaching function. In order to satisfy the needs of Xers, we will need to do both. But how far should we take this role of information provider? Mood (1994) goes so far as to suggest that patrons could leave a request and come back at a later time to find a "neatly organized file of material, compiled just for his or her search," consisting of a printout of citations on the subject and possibly downloaded documents from full-text databases, photocopies of articles, and relevant books on the topic. Generation X, as well as many other students and faculty, would welcome this level of service, but most libraries do not have the resources necessary to make this a reality.

What we can do is anticipate the needs of our patrons and make available practical guides in the form of neat, concise, laser-printed handouts. We can redesign the traditional pathfinders and bibliographies to be more appealing to Xers. Limit handouts to one page of the most practical information. Avoid long, narrative descriptions, opting instead for brevity. Strive for attractiveness and readability, in addition to usefulness and currency. Use headings, subheadings, and bullets to get and keep Xers' attention. Prepare handouts in response to the most frequently asked questions: a list of job ad sites on the Net, a fact sheet on internships, an overview of opportunities and directories for the environmentally-concerned student, etc. Review publications frequently for outdated information and needed updates. Make handouts available where students want them. Forget the neat display in the circulation area if students are asking for this information in Reference or at the Career Development office. Distribute this pre-packaged information in as many alternative ways as possible–in the campus newspaper, on the OPAC, via e-mail and FAX on request, and in the residence halls.

In the process of streamlining to be more efficient and cost-effective, it is sometimes easy for libraries to consider withdrawing one on one services in favor of group programs and instruction; however, Xers' need for quick information and personal contact suggests that we need to continue providing professional reference and instructional services on demand. Reference by appointment is an excellent way to meet their need for personal attention, but not at the expense of having a professional at the reference desk when they need one. Planned group instruction will reach some students, but not the majority of Xers who will expect individual instruction on a need-to-know basis.

COLLECTIONS

The focus so far has been on services rather than collections for job seekers. The characteristics of Generation X students should prompt us to reevaluate our collection development policies. Instead of purchasing a wide variety of expensive business directories on a three-year cycle, consider keeping only the most useful and popular ones and updating those annually. Better yet, in addition, purchase business CD-ROMs which suply full-text articles that can instantly be printed when they are found, instead of having to search through the periodicals stacks for back issues in order to make photocopies. Avoid holding on to or directing students toward "classic" job search or job preparation materials. What's a classic to us will immediately be suspect to students as outdated and irrelevant to them. Xers expect the most up-to-date information.

Collections or guides to the collection should also be located where students are most likely to look for the information. Abel (1992, p. 57) hits on a common frustration of job hunting Xers who are both "unaware and reluctant to utilize the somewhat scattered resource base" found at most universities. The result may be the establishment of a Career Planning Information Center, as happened at DePaul University, or some other means of making career resources more centrally available to users.

PERSONNEL

The suggestions which appear here are based on the premise that Xers, in general, are not crazy about libraries. They would prefer to conduct all of their job search research from their home or the computer lab. If this were completely true, we could embrace Campbell's (1992) goal of answering "no less than 75 percent of the questions that currently come to our reference desks using computers . . . without human intervention" (31). There is, however, at least one overwhelming reason why we shouldn't plan on locking the library doors just yet. Maximizing convenience by utilizing FAX, E-mail, and distance learning technologies does not minimize an Xers' need for personal contact. Cannon found universally, with each and every focus group that he conducted, that Xers were impressed by people and organizations which they felt cared about them. Students look for caring in facial expressions, eye contact, body language, verbal cues such as welcoming greetings and use of personal names, and the general physical appearances of staff and facilities. Xers highly value personal contacts and retain vivid impressions of interactions and surroundings. For us, this means that our public service areas should be staffed with librarians who genuinely enjoy working with students. All employees could benefit from staff development programs focusing on these basic interpersonal skills because it is unrealistic to think that computers will eliminate the need for personal contact in the near future.

Another way that we can meet the needs of attention-hungry Xers would be to establish or strengthen departmental liaison programs. To serve job seeking Xers, this means having a librarian liaison to the campus career development office. This librarian would have normal liaison responsibilities for collection development, bibliography, and library instruction in the areas of career planning and placement. In a recent survey, Abel (1992) discovered that there is very little organized communication between career planning departments and libraries and that "rarely" did one department refer to another's resources or services in more than just "a passing way." This could be remedied by assigning such a liaison and establishing a referral process between the two departments. This gives Xers the personal attention and contact they crave as well as identifying this liaison librarian as an "expert" on library career planning resources. Xers admire and will seek out expertise in their area of need or interest.

CONCLUSION

There is ongoing debate about whether the characteristics outlined and discussed above concerning Generation X are actually unique to this current generation or are simply the characteristics of young people in general, regardless of their generation. Certainly universals exist; however, we must recognize the real cultural differences resulting from the environment in which Generation X grew up. We should be aware of their affinity for and familiarity with technology, their acceptance of diversity, their savvy consumerism, as well as their expectations for instant gratification. Attempts to define the character of a generation may be perceived negatively as stereotyping or labelling, but such information can be useful to consider when looking ahead and planning for change.

REFERENCES

Abel, C. (1992). A survey of cooperative activities between career planning departments and academic libraries. In *Library services for career planning, job searching, and employment opportunities.* Byron Anderson, ed. Binghamton, NY: The Haworth Press, Inc.
Campbell, J.D. (1992). Shaking the conceptual foundations of reference: A perspective, Reference Services Review, 20(4): 29-36.

Cannon, D. (1991). Generation X: The way they do the things they do. *Journal of Career Planning and Employment,* 51(2): 34-38.

Cannon, D. (1994). *Generation X and the new work ethic.* London: Demos.

Coupland, D. (1991). *Generation X: Tales for an accelerated culture.* New York: St. Martin's.

Dey, E.L., Astin, A.W. & Korn, W.S. (1991). *The American freshman: Twenty-five year trends, 1966-1990.* (ERIC Document ED 340 325).

Mood, T.A. (1994). Of sundials and digital watches: A further step toward the new paradigm of reference. *Reference Services Review,* 22(3): 27-32, 95.

Strauss, W. & Howe, N. (1991). *Generations: The history of America's future, 1584-2069.* New York: Morrow.

The Liberal Arts Job Search in an Electronic Environment: The Founding and Development of Alumnae Resources

Bonnie Willdorf

SUMMARY. What began as a career networking support group in the living room of a visionary Smith College alumna has grown into a nationally recognized, independent nonprofit career development organization. Today Alumnae Resources provides a comprehensive range of services to thousands of college-educated women and men, most with liberal arts backgrounds. AR's career development model focuses on the need for information, and as the organization has grown and advanced technologically, so has its core, the Resource Center. The library now provides a variety of electronic tools for individual career research. Though some may be intimidated by this electronic environment, their education can be an advantage in adapting to the new technology and succeeding in the changing workplace. *[Article copies available from The Haworth Document Delivery Service: 1-800-342-9678. E-mail address: getinfo@haworth.com]*

INTRODUCTION

The electronic environment that existed when Alumnae Resources was formed in the mid-1970's had its basis in telephones,

---

Bonnie Willdorf is Resource Center Director, Alumnae Resources, 120 Montgomery Street, Suite 600, San Francisco, CA 94104, and is a member of the American Library Association and the Special Libraries Association.

[Haworth co-indexing entry note]: "The Liberal Arts Job Search in an Electronic Environment: The Founding and Development of Alumnae Resources." Willdorf, Bonnie. Co-published simultaneously in *The Reference Librarian* (The Haworth Press, Inc.) No. 55, 1996, pp. 61-71; and: *Career Planning and Job Searching in the Information Age* (ed: Elizabeth A. Lorenzen) The Haworth Press, Inc., 1996, pp. 61-71. Single or multiple copies of this article are available from The Haworth Document Delivery Service [1-800-342-9678, 9:00 a.m. - 5:00 p.m. (EST). E-mail address: getinfo@haworth.com].

not computers, and the "networking" that AR's founder, Glady Thacher, speaks about had nothing to do with LANs or the Internet. Glady Thacher had already founded one major nonprofit organization in San Francisco, Enterprise for High School Students, when she was asked to be an alumna member of the Smith College Board of Directors in 1972. The offer was interesting, but she wanted to be a more active participant in the life of the alumnae, particularly since at the time many local Smith clubs were moribund.

Glady felt that it would be worthwhile to look at Smith graduates, assess their needs, both personal and professional, and then work to form a network of support for one another. Since most Smith grads were liberal arts majors and had, after graduation, devoted their time to family and community, they had been left out of the loop of careers and the business world. Even the recent graduates at that time had not had any significant career counseling in college.

The vision that Glady Thacher had for Alumnae Resources (which was originally founded as Smith Resources) was for a network of women who would be resources to each other in the job search – they would help each other to get into professional careers. She realized that the career search is a time of transition, a time which requires thoughtfulness, understanding and patience. The essence of her insight was that the quest to find a job or develop a career is a non-linear, ongoing process, and that during this process, people need support, assistance and, most of all, *information*. They need information to assess their own skills and values, to be knowledgeable about the economy and available career options, to strategize and implement a job search, and to continue advancing in their field or look at new career directions. These principles that the founder of Alumnae Resources espoused in the mid-1970's are still the backbone of this independent nonprofit organization.

A RESOURCE CENTER IS BORN

When Glady and her friends in the San Francisco Smith Club founded Smith Resources, they set the stage for the library (which is known as the Resource Center at AR) that exists now. They sent out questionnaires to the approximately 1400 Smith graduates in the San Francisco Bay Area with two queries:

- What did you do in college?
- What are you doing now?

The 500 returned questionnaires were compiled into "Opportunity Books" in Glady's living room (where the organization existed for several years). When a Smith graduate came by, she could look through these books and be inspired, for instance, by seeing information about a woman with a major similar to hers (e.g., economics) who was now working in a field such as theater arts. Now, Alumnae Resources has a Career Advisor Network of over 1000 professionals in the San Francisco Bay Area who give informational interviews to its 7000 members. AR's library houses the Advisors' resume's, which are in binders just like Glady's Opportunity Books, but all of their biographical information and the sign-out system for arranging interviews are computerized.

ALUMNAE RESOURCES GROWS

There have been many other changes since Alumnae Resources began in Glady Thacher's living room. The organization has seen phenomenal growth since its incorporation in 1979 (see Figure 1). Membership has increased from 35 to 7000. Client visits to the Resource Center are approaching 1500 people per week. AR has existed in three locations, each much larger than the previous one; in the Spring of 1995 it moved into its fourth, 15,500 sq. ft. in a Financial District building, which doubled the size of the Resource Center in order to accommodate the exponential growth in client visits that is expected in the coming years.

AR'S MEMBERSHIP PROGRAM

Today, Alumnae Resources provides a comprehensive range of services to both women and men who are seeking to begin, advance or change their careers. These services include individual career counseling, workshops, panels, support groups and, at the core of this vital network of resources, the career library.

FIGURE 1

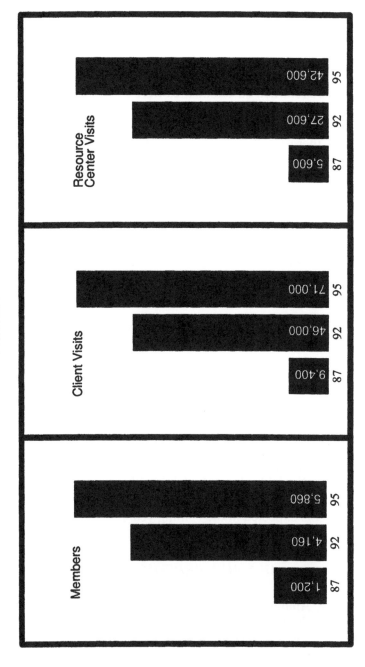

Individual memberships cost $75 per year and entitle members to numerous free benefits, including:

- Job Listings on CareerLine–A touch-tone connection to employer-recorded job listings
- Employer Forum–A series in which selected companies make short presentations about their organizations and the benefits they offer to prospective employees.
- Survival Skills Series–Three introductory workshops designed to give job seekers the basic skills to survive during unemployment.
- Job Clubs–Weekly support groups led by career counselors for members actively seeking jobs.
- Women of Color, Networking/Support Groups–Three professionally led support groups for Latina and Native American, Asian American and African American women.
- Newsletter/Calendar–Subscription to Alumnae Resources' quarterly publication of news and catalog of workshops
- Unlimited use of the Resource Center, which contains career research materials, job listings and labor market information.

Alumnae Resources' programs, which began as a single resume-writing seminar, now consist of over 650 workshops, seminars and career panels each year. The program of workshops is designed around the four phases of the career development process:

- Phase I–Self-Assessment: A self-assessment of skills, values, interests and personality type.
- Phase II–Exploring Career Options: Based on a clearer focus of one's own skills and values, one explores realistic career options through informational interviewing, networking, research, seminars and career panels.
- Phase III–Planning a Strategy: With the focus gained from self-assessment and exploration of new options, a strategy for targeting and obtaining a new job is planned.
- Phase IV–Professional Development: As individuals progress in their fields they continuously need to gain new skills and expertise to remain marketable and for their own personal growth and satisfaction.

Alumnae Resources offers workshops to guide individuals through each of these four phases. For people approaching the beginning of the process, the basic, five-week "Self-Assessment" workshop, taught by licensed career counselors, is one of the most popular—there are currently 26 separate sections of this course. The workshop is intensive and leads clients through a comprehensive series of exercises and diagnostic instruments to help them clarify past accomplishments, skills, values, interests and personality.

Phase II classes include "The Next Step," a three-week workshop that takes members into the Resource Center and teaches them how to begin researching careers and industries. AR also offers workshops on specific career fields such as "Careers in the Visual Arts," "The Multimedia Industry," and "Fundraising Careers," and twelve career panels each quarter which feature four women talking about their careers in a particular field such as advertising, training, human resources, or multimedia.

For those who have moved into Phase III, Alumnae Resources has workshops on writing a resume, networking, interviewing, working with an executive recruiter, and how to tap into the hidden job market. Career Strategy Groups are also offered which allow members to work directly with a career counselor in small groups of eight to set goals, strategize and avoid the isolation and depression so endemic to the job search.

AR members also have the ability to acquire up-to-the minute information about job searching in the electronic age through the three hour workshop entitled "Marketing Yourself Using Your Home Computer," which explores electronic networking, the Internet, electronic bulletin boards and job listing services, database research, contact management software, mail merging cover letters, faxing from home, "uploading" your resume, resume scanning systems and more. This workshop was first presented to the Alumnae Resources staff in the fall of 1994 so that all could be familiar with the nomenclature and capabilities of "what's out there," and thus be of more help to clients.

Phase IV, Professional Development, features a wide array of workshops to meet the needs of individuals who want to acquire new skills or manage the increasing demands of the ever-changing job market. These offerings include "Assertive Communication,"

"Career Development Strategies for African-American Women," "Asking the Right Questions," "Time Management," "Managing Your Personal Finances," and "Expertise: Staying Competitive in the 90's."

DEVELOPMENT OF THE RESOURCE CENTER

Clearly, Glady Thacher's vision of a place where college-educated women could find information and support to pursue their career search is reflected in Alumnae Resources' present counseling and workshop program. But at the core of this vision was the idea that many people, especially those with a liberal arts background, would need the opportunity to assess their skills through introspection, and then do their own research to determine their career direction–to put it simply, they would need a library. As AR developed, the importance of its Resource Center grew with it.

In 1984, the Resource Center consisted of one two-drawer file cabinet and one small bookshelf in the corner of the entryway of the four tiny rooms that were Alumnae Resources. This original office, opened in 1981, was in a funky building on downtown San Francisco's Mission Street. A move to larger quarters, still in a funky building, still on Mission Street, in 1985 enabled the Resource Center to be substantially expanded. Now it was in a 1600 sq. ft. room which was used as a library, workshop room and orientation room. Eight large bookcases and three file cabinets were purchased. The most significant change here, though, was that there was a place for people to come and do their research, with actual tables and chairs for their comfort and convenience. Materials were purchased with a small budget and donations were solicited.

Today, the Resource Center contains over 1300 books organized in 50 color-coded categories, and more than 4000 files on local companies, nonprofit organizations, professional associations, various career issues, industries and occupations. There are subscriptions to more than 100 serials, many of which are job listings periodicals; in addition there are 80 binders which contain thousands of job listings from local companies and organizations.

Members can use the SearchMAGIC database system to obtain information about virtually all of the materials in the library. F&S

Index Plus Text is available on InfoTrac, and there are plans for more CD-ROM subscriptions as the budget allows.

The Resource Center's files are filled with the results of the many hours of clipping that the staff does every week. Though it would be ideal to forgo this labor-intensive process in favor of electronic data, there are several reasons why that is not currently feasible. First, full-text CD-ROM sources are few, and they are expensive. Second, in order to contain costs, experienced on-line searchers would be needed rather than allowing members to do the research themselves, which would go against AR's principle of career self-reliance. (The thought of allowing AR's highly-educated but inexperienced members into a source such as Dialog can send chills up a director's budgetary spine). Third, the current system gives members an edge–if Resource Center staff members clip from the papers on a daily or weekly basis, the information is available in a much more timely fashion than a CD-ROM which is, at best, a month behind. In the not-too-distant future, though, more electronic applications for searching company and industry information, e.g., annual reports, should become available.

The Resource Center is also home to the aforementioned Career Advisor Network and its automated check-out system, as well as several Macintoshs and a PC available for member rental. Two copy machines are located in the library for member use, and fax resumes and cover letters can be faxed anywhere in the world for a reasonable price.

ELECTRONIC APPLICATIONS IN THE RESOURCE CENTER AND THE ORGANIZATION

It is sometimes hard to believe that less than five years ago, the only electronic application in the Resource Center was an electric typewriter. There was a very basic card catalog (title and author entries only), and a typed alphabetical-only index to the files. The Career Advisor Network (CAN) signout system, used to track all AR members qualified to use the network and schedule informational interviews, was completely manual. That was the Dark Ages, yet there were many AR members, and staff, who were very comfortable in that environment.

Progress, of course, was inevitable. By the beginning of 1991, the library had been computerized for word processing, and a CAN signout program had been installed which was linked to the organization's membership database. In 1993, Alumnae Resources made a quantum leap in its technology. It invested in a state-of-the-art constituent database, Raiser's Edge™, re-configuring over 25,000 records for the new system, converting the CAN portion of the old database to FoxPro and creating a bridge facility for daily data transfer from one database to the other.

That same year, AR purchased InMAGIC software and developed its database structures to include all of the books, serials, files, college catalogs and job listings, which are entered into this database and are available to members via SearchMAGIC, the public access component. For instance, if a member is curious as to how many environmental jobs have been posted in the Resource Center in the past month, SearchMAGIC will give her that information in seconds. If a member wants to know how many management consulting firms or nonprofits that deal with youth issues are on file, or the names of professional associations in the broadcasting field, SearchMAGIC can tell her instantly. Subject searches that bring up all formats (books, serials, files) can be accomplished quickly. All serials management and ordering is also accomplished through InMAGIC.

A unique list of subject headings based more on career development models than on LC was developed. These are constantly being revised as new industries, for example multimedia, come into being.

These technologically advanced systems have expanded AR's available information resources, and enabled AR staff to have much better access to this collection, but has this helped its members? In fact, it appears that many people are still intimidated by computers. They know that in the current workplace, there are fewer and fewer jobs which do not require some familiarity with computers, but to some people, particularly women with liberal arts backgrounds, and of a generation that did not grow up in the Information Age, becoming computer-conversant can be a terrifying prospect. These individuals may think that it means having to somehow transform themselves into "techies," rather than simply becoming comfortable with computers and understanding what powerful tools they can be, particularly, of course, in libraries.

To help AR's clients bridge this gap in perspective, some instructional initiatives have taken place, and there are plans for more. Handouts and simple directions for using SearchMAGIC have been developed; in the future, a regularly scheduled Resource Center Orientation, with interactive teaching aids that will demonstrate the awesome power of SearchMAGIC, and its "user-friendliness" as well, will be offered.

The recently initiated telephone job hotline and information service, CareerLine, represents another milestone in AR's services. Any member with access to a touch-tone telephone can tap this computerized information resource from remote locations. Employers can dial in to record their own job openings and post them at their convenience, and members can call 24 hours a day, 7 days a week to hear job listings in their fields of interest. A touch-tone menu system prompts new callers and helps them locate topics of interest, while repeat callers can go directly to specific job categories or get daily updates of new listings if they wish.

Though some of AR's clients may have minimal experience with computers, a large percentage (over 50%) do own or have access to a computer with a modem line. Alumnae Resources' goal is to expand its services and make them available to all members who wish to learn how to use these resources or increase their facility in accessing them. AR's Newsletter/Calendar, including classes, career panels and events, is posted each quarter on the Women's Wire service.

Alumnae Resources now has its own domain on the Internet, through which forums and postings of organizational interest can be accessed. This facilitates communication with board members, vendors, instructors and members. Job listings are also received from Human Resources departments that prefer to distribute such information electronically. By the end of 1995, there are plans to offer more information services on either a private forum on the World Wide Web or on AR's own electronic bulletin board. A number of provider systems are currently being evaluated, primarily for user-friendly interface and labor and cost effectiveness. Such a forum would allow members to be provided with remote access to the SearchMAGIC library catalog, job opportunities, conferences on workplace issues, the Career Advisor Network, test taking and other services. For members who are already "hooked into" the Internet, the Resource

Center provides a handout of the ever-growing and changing list of employment resources that are available on the Internet.

In addition, Alumnae Resources is working with local public library systems so that their on-line systems can be accessed. The San Francisco Public Library and Alameda County Library System will also both be providing some type of yet-to-be determined access to AR's on-line resources as they develop.

CONCLUSION: LIBERAL ARTS JOB SEARCH AND THE NEW WORKPLACE MODEL

The world of work is changing. William Bridges has written in *JobShift: How to Prosper in a Workplace Without Jobs* (Addison-Wesley Publishing Company, 1994): *"Today's workers need to forget jobs completely and look instead for work that needs doing—and then set themselves up as the best way to get that work done."* Project work rather than jobs—this paradigm shift occurring in the economy affects the way people must view themselves and the methods they must use to manage their careers. And just as the individual who wishes to be successful needs not only to adapt to change but to anticipate it, so must the successful organization. Alumnae Resources understands that if it fails to keep up with the changes in the world of work or the changes in the way information is transmitted, it will become irrelevant. Thus, through the development of workshops, career counseling, resources and systems, it is engaged in an ongoing process to grow with the times, so that it can assist its clients in the same process. It is clear that the skills that people will need to thrive in this changing workplace certainly will include knowledge of and ability to navigate in the electronic world.

People with liberal arts backgrounds have, perhaps, an advantage in this environment. Being generalists rather than specialists is what may give them the edge over those with a more narrowly focused education. The skills developed in college, and the broader understanding of the forces at work in society, will prepare them to position themselves even more competitively in the new workplace model.

IV. COLLABORATIVE EFFORTS

Job Search Strategies: Library Instruction Collaborates with University Career Services

Brian DeHart

SUMMARY. Collaboration between the academic library and the university placement office is a natural partnership. Joint planning and consultation in both collection development and programming evolve into more ambitious endeavors such as instruction. At DePaul University, this relationship has become well established through the efforts of library administration and reference/instruction librarians. The combined effort has resulted in students' increased use of library resources in order to prepare better for the job market, while gaining life-long skills for finding and analyzing career information. *[Article copies available from The Haworth Document Delivery Service: 1-800-342-9678. E-mail address: getinfo@haworth.com]*

Brian DeHart is Reference/Instruction Librarian, DePaul University Library, Loop Campus, 1 East Jackson, Chicago, IL 60604.

[Haworth co-indexing entry note]: "Job Search Strategies: Library Instruction Collaborates with University Career Services." DeHart, Brian. Co-published simultaneously in *The Reference Librarian* (The Haworth Press, Inc.) No. 55, 1996, pp. 73-81; and: *Career Planning and Job Searching in the Information Age* (ed: Elizabeth A. Lorenzen) The Haworth Press, Inc., 1996, pp. 73-81. Single or multiple copies of this article are available from The Haworth Document Delivery Service [1-800-342-9678, 9:00 a.m. - 5:00 p.m. (EST). E-mail address: getinfo@haworth.com].

INTRODUCTION

The academic library and the university placement office can serve students more effectively by pooling resources and utilizing each other's strengths. Despite this fact, Abel's survey from 1992 of fifty institutions showed a general lack of substantive cooperative efforts, while respondents acknowledged they could do more.[1] Of course, situations will vary in both departments according to staff members' talents, philosophies, administrative policies, and budgeting. Even the most modest attempts at collaboration, however, can grow into well established and successful programs.

Traditional library resources such as business directories and periodicals offer a wealth of insight into company activities and industry background. Increasingly, these resources are available in electronic formats accessible through CD-ROM or via the Internet. As librarians work in an ever evolving world of information, they are best positioned to instruct students about how these resources, both in print and electronic formats, interact with each other. On the other hand, professional career counselors are better able to assess individual students' career needs and to provide appropriate vocational guidance. In addition, through the services of a university placement office, students have access to alumni and corporate networks. A combination of these two departments' resources, rather than one alone, prepares a student well for the job search and gives him or her a competitive edge in identifying and obtaining a satisfying job.

LIBRARY RESOURCES AND THE JOB SEARCH

DePaul University Library, in cooperation with the university's placement office (called the Career Development Center) has provided for several years a Career Information Center (CIC). There is a CIC located within the John T. Richardson Library at the Lincoln Park campus and in the Loop Campus Library in DePaul Center. Each CIC is housed in a separate room immediately adjacent to the reference desk, providing a central location for books, videos, and periodicals on all aspects of career planning. The glass walled room gives the CIC an identity separate from the reference collection while still offering patrons ready access to reference assistance.

The CIC collection is tailored to the specific needs and programs of each DePaul campus. The Lincoln Park campus is the site of most liberal arts, natural sciences, health sciences, and performing arts classes; its CIC has been developed with these subjects in mind. The Loop Campus is home to the College of Commerce, the College of Computer Science and the adult student program, the School for New Learning. Thus, the CIC in the Loop Campus Library reflects the needs of business and computer science graduates and career changers, respectively. Each CIC contains a personal computer with access to the online catalog, SIGI+ career interest assessment software, and GRE Graduate School Selector. All materials can be found in the online catalog. Selected print and video titles may be borrowed for a one week period.

Researching a company is vital for a successful job search. Career counselors and recruiters universally agree on this statement, yet many job seekers fail to appreciate its importance.[2] Most recruiters say that the interest and enthusiasm for the company that a job candidate brings to the interview strongly influences their decision about the candidate. From the candidate's perspective, the process of gathering information on a company helps to answer the question, "Do I want to work for this business or institution?" Many job seekers overlook this step as a means of preparing for an interview. They then spend interview time asking questions about the company when they should be selling themselves as future employees of that company.

JOB SEARCH INSTRUCTION

According to Wu et al., "knowing the context in which an academic library operates and conveying what informational resources and services a library can offer to its varied constituencies are keys to the success of a library as a fully integrated part of the academic enterprise."[3] The first step toward a successful collaboration between the academic library and the placement office is to establish a rapport among staff and to identify the team members. Effective use of this relationship requires:

- Taking advantage of a counselor's exposure to professional contacts and literature by inviting suggestions for collection development.
- Educating placement office staff about career relevant resources, both in print and electronic formats, as they become available.
- Inquiring about student needs and how the library can better serve those needs.

Once this relationship is established, working together on programs can become a natural extension. One of those programs might be instruction on using the library resources during the job search process.

An early step toward instruction on career-related resources in the DePaul University Library took the form of a pathfinder. Still in use, it is designed to show which directories and other resources contain information on companies scheduled for on-campus interviews. At the beginning of each academic quarter, a librarian researches companies listed in the *On-Campus Recruiting Schedule* prepared by the Career Development Center. A strategy sheet is created for each company which is then filed in a binder shelved in the CIC. Since many of the companies return on a regular basis, only a handful of new strategy sheets needs to be added each quarter. A quick scan of the weekly *On-Campus Recruiting Schedule* identifies newly added companies and strategy sheets are promptly created for them.

The top of each strategy sheet indicates whether the company is private, public, or a subsidiary. This is important for establishing realistic expectations about the amount of company information generally available.[4] The following scenarios demonstrate some of the "unrealistic" expectations students might have about company information:

- Equate being incorporated with being a public company;
- Assume corporate annual reports are available for one of the Big Six accounting firms, all of which are private and not subject to disclosure laws;

* Become frustrated when no specific information exists, not even a directory entry, on a small, local, and private marketing firm.

In the absence of a librarian, the strategy sheets serve as a basic, independent guide to the resources relevant to company research available at DePaul Library. The call numbers of useful directories and other reference titles are indicated, giving students an efficient start to their research. With a librarian at a student's side, the strategy sheets lay the foundation for more in depth research, particularly in regards to electronic resources.

Each strategy sheet ends with the suggestion that students search electronic indexes for relevant articles on the company and/or its industry as a whole (See Figure 1). Electronic indexes are indispensable for quickly identifying recent articles about a company's activities by allowing the researcher to search using a company name field. Industry trends can be gleaned in those databases that permit searching by Standard Industrial Classification (SIC) code. The DePaul Library provides access to several databases that job seekers find particularly useful for their business content.[5] *ABI/Inform, Compact Disclosure, Newspaper Abstracts,* and *Predicasts F&S Index* are all accessible on the university's wide area network. Students can also search *Business Periodicals Index* through the Illinois Bibliographic Information Service (IBIS) available via ILLINET Online, the statewide resource-sharing network.

In a best case scenario, a student researching a publicly held company will be able to locate financial data and recent articles about the company. At the very least, the researcher should come away with a sense of the industry in which the company operates. Often this is the only option when smaller, private companies escape the notice of directories and the periodical literature.

COLLABORATIVE JOB SEARCH SEMINARS

The DePaul University Library has developed an integrated program of library instruction over the last several years. Library instruction is effectively presented not only in appropriate courses, but at the appropriate time within a course to maximize learning and

FIGURE 1

Castle Metals

When researching this company, see also listings for: **A.M. Castle** (official name)

This company, or its parent company, is publicly owned and listed on the American Stock Exchange. Annual reports and 10-K reports may be available in the Loop Campus Library—inquire at the reference desk.

Some suggested sources of information:

- *Ward's Business Directory*
  R.338.74W267aa (LC Reference Desk)

- *Moody's Industrial Manual*
  R.332.6M817 (LC)

- *International Directory of Company Histories*
  R.338.7409I61s (LC)

- *Job Seeker's Guide to Private and Public Companies*
  R.331J62g (LC,LP Career Information Center)

- *The Career Guide: Dun's Employment Opportunities Directory*
  R.331.12D926 (LC,LP Career Information Center)

- Automated Reference Center databases may provide relevant citations to articles about the company appearing in journals, magazines, newsletters, and/or newspapers.

  ABI/Inform
  Predicasts F&S Index
  Newspaper Abstracts
  etc.

PLEASE CONSULT WITH A REFERENCE LIBRARIAN IF YOU HAVE ANY QUESTIONS.

reinforcement. Job search instruction has been similarly assimilated into the job search seminars sponsored by the university's Career Development Center (CDC). In the past, the Library has held workshops for students on the methods of researching a company prior to interviewing. Unfortunately, these sessions on how to research companies suffered from poor attendance despite different methods of promotion ranging from the posting of flyers at strategic campus locations to direct referrals. When the CDC began offering its own series of job search seminars, the Library approached them about combining instructional efforts and developing a unified presentation for this stage in the students' interview preparation.

The Library's independent workshop was subsequently condensed to fit within the framework of the CDC seminars. The library component addresses the generally recognized steps toward compiling a company profile and the resources associated with each step[6] (See Figure 2). The need for flexibility in the process is stressed; the direction taken and the resources consulted will depend on the individual's needs and situation. Reference sources are also highlighted in a multipage handout that provides a text for participants to follow and keep for future use. Holding the seminars in the CDC offices offers three distinct advantages for the library:

- The students do not necessarily expect to encounter a librarian outside of the library, thus their interest is piqued;
- The library presentation receives an introduction by and the full support of the career counselor;
- The library, when discussed in the physical surroundings of the placement office, is perceived as an integral part of the job search process.

Time allotment in the seminars is one of the concessions made between the Library and the CDC. Current practice has the librarian speak for approximately one half hour in the middle of a two hour CDC seminar. This obviously does not allow enough time for a demonstration of even one electronic business index. The time can be better utilized describing the *research process,* rather than delivering a barrage of details describing individual reference products. One suggestion would be to offer separate workshops of a general nature devoted to hands-on demonstration of electronic resources. These can serve to attract any student sincerely interested in learning more about the details of specific products while not boring those in attendance already familiar with them.

Student feedback has been positive since initiating these joint job search seminars. Many express surprise that a Career Information

FIGURE 2. Search Strategy Flowchart

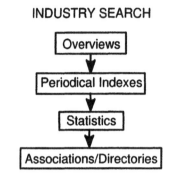

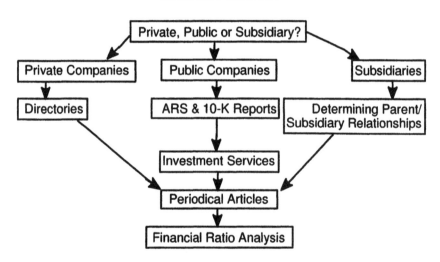

Center exists within the library. Invariably, several of those attending the seminar are seen using the library in the days immediately following. Evening MBA students have been particularly appreciative. Since they work full-time and often have family obligations, time is of the essence. Few have stopped to explore the library and the depth of its collection. The value of the library stands out more to these students when it is explained in the context of career planning and placement.

CONCLUSION

This cooperative effort between the university library and the placement office can create a win-win situation, not only for the library and the placement office, but also for the students. The career information collections within the DePaul University Library are well used by patrons. Many students are referred to the Library by the CDC and vice versa. Students approach the placement office with a specific purpose in mind—to find a job upon graduation. The job search seminar creates a ready market for library instruction. The professional CDC counselor directing the seminar underscores the importance of librarians and other library resources in learning about a company or industry as the first step in getting a job. The goal is to make students aware of resources they might otherwise overlook as they enter the job search. No claim is made that these efforts have a direct quantitative effect on the hiring of DePaul graduates. In a tight job market, collaboration provides students with an advantage, albeit intangible. It is they who ultimately will benefit.

REFERENCES

1. Abel, Charlene. "A Survey of Cooperative Activities Between Career Planning Departments and Academic Libraries," *The Reference Librarian,* no. 36, 51-60.

2. Lafevre, John, *How You Really Get Hired,* New York: Prentice Hall, 1992, 22.

3. Wu, Connie et al., "Effective Liaison Relationships in an Academic Library," *College and Research Libraries News,* 55, no. 5 (May 1994): 254, 303.

4. Crowther, Karmen N.T. *Researching Your Way to a Good Job,* New York: John Wiley, 1993, 11.

5. Fries, James R. and Dow, Ronald R., "New CD-ROM Technologies Help the Unemployed Search for Jobs," *American Libraries,* 23, no. 10 (November 1992): 845-848.

6. Hawbaker, Craig A. and Nixon, Judith M. *Industry and Company Information: Illustrated Search Strategy and Sources.* Ann Arbor, MI: Pierian Press, 1991.

Developing a Career Information Gopher: The University of Michigan Experience

Jeanne E. Miller

SUMMARY. The Career Planning and Placement Office at the University of Michigan designed and implemented a career information gopher as part of its move toward a 24-hour office. This article investigates conceptual issues regarding the organization and delivery of information in the career area. It also reviews the process of arranging career information for electronic delivery, integrating customer service and information provision concerns with the advantages and limitations of the gopher structure and format, and planning for ongoing maintenance of the gopher information. *[Article copies available from The Haworth Document Delivery Service: 1-800-342-9678. E-mail address: getinfo@haworth.com]*

INTRODUCTION

The University of Michigan Career Planning and Placement Office designed and mounted a gopher within the University of Michigan's GOpher BLUE server in 1994. From development through implementation, the gopher design process reflected questions about such subjects as the organization of career information, methods and issues in delivering information to students through elec-

Jeanne E. Miller is Librarian, Career Planning and Placement Office, University of Michigan, 3200 SAB 515 E. Jefferson St., Ann Arbor, MI 48109-1316.

Gopher Task Force members included Sherri Carillo, Angie Hall, Mariella Mecozzi, and Simone Himbeault Taylor.

[Haworth co-indexing entry note]: "Developing a Career Information Gopher: The University of Michigan Experience." Miller, Jeanne E. Co-published simultaneously in *The Reference Librarian* (The Haworth Press, Inc) No. 55, 1996, pp. 83-97; and: *Career Planning and Job Searching in the Information Age* (ed: Elizabeth A. Lorenzen) The Haworth Press, Inc., 1996, pp. 83-97. Single or multiple copies of this article are available from The Haworth Document Delivery Service [1-800-342-9678, 9:00 a.m. - 5:00 p.m. (EST). E-mail address: getinfo@haworth.com].

83

tronic means, and transferring information currently in print and other formats into electronically user-friendly formats. The CP&P gopher also offered a means to advance the goal of having a 24 hour office and tapping into the resources and directions of the University of Michigan. As a process, the development of this gopher provided career and information professionals with a unique opportunity to revisit the conceptual and organizational underpinnings of the arrangement of career information. Finally, the gopher project allowed the organization to put into place a mechanism for information delivery that in itself reflects the technological world for which its users are preparing.

PURPOSE AND GOALS OF THE CAREER PLANNING AND PLACEMENT GOPHER

The University of Michigan Career Planning and Placement Office (CP&P) is one of several career offices on Michigan's Ann Arbor campus but, as a unit of the Division of Student Affairs, is the only comprehensive office, serving students from all schools and colleges at the University, from first year students through graduate students and alumni/ae. The culture of the University of Michigan strongly supports student computer use: an ample number of computers using Macintosh, DOS, and UNIX platforms are readily available across campus for student use; bulletin boards and user groups are incorporated into many classes; and the UM-GOpher BLUE gopher serves as a site for information about specific offices, library resources, and city information. The decision to undertake development of the CP&P gopher joined CP&P goals with University trends.

In 1992, Career Planning and Placement developed a strategic plan and 2 years later participated in a Student Affairs-wide self assessment based on the Council for the Advancement of Standards (CAS) guidelines. Each of these self-evaluations highlighted information delivery as a strength of the office as well as a future direction. Specifically, one of the two themes in the 1992 strategic plan stated that, "CP&P will provide dynamic career information to schools, colleges, and other units to assist them in their work with students."[1] More recently, the Action Plan section of the CAS self-assessment includes under the heading of enhancement, "Become the 'office without walls,' the 24 hour career office."[2] The concept of the "office without walls" or the "24 hour office" is one that CP&P has been working toward for the past few years. Extended service hours and an increase in campus-wide dissemination of services had led to higher customer satisfaction, but the University of Michigan student body increasingly uses technology to perform a host of daily activities. Furthermore, students want access when they are interested in acquiring information—and student schedules seldom match normal business hours. In addition, alumni/ae clients present an increased demand for services, due to the weakening economy of the past few years. For this customer group, coming into the office is frequently difficult or impossible.

The office decided to mount a Career Planning and Placement Gopher on the University's GOpher BLUE server in order to make available information about the wide range of services, programs, and resources in a format that provides not simply "just in time" information, but "just for you" information. This technological venture was in addition to existing hard copy information resources (e.g., a program brochure each semester, an annual mailing to sophomores and seniors highlighting services and resources of special interest to them, and flyers, bibliographies, info-paks and handouts), and initially was seen as an electronic version of such products available to students, alumni/ae and others on a 24 hour basis. To develop this gopher, an internal cross-functional team formed, consisting of the librarian, the systems analyst, an assistant director as the career development expert, the manager of the reference letter service and the Director of the office.

CONCEPTUAL AND PHILOSOPHICAL DESIGN ISSUES

Before beginning the design process, the team wrestled with several issues that were necessary as a foundation for the gopher design process.

- How will the gopher be used by clients?
- What sorts of information are best suited to electronic format?
- What type of information should be provided (e.g., complete information or leads to the office)?

- What format should be used for information: Full text? Forms? Informational lists?
- How should the information demands of the 24 hour office/office without walls be balanced with concerns about counseling ethics and counseling needs?
- How do we ensure that the gopher maintains our high standards of customer service?

Several of these concerns were interrelated. For example, there was a concern that offering the full text of some documents might present ethical issues regarding use. As a theory driven office, counseling is considered one of a range of approaches used to assist students in their career development. If students found information on the gopher and felt they had "all the facts" would they, in essence, dismiss the one-on-one opportunity that might better meet their needs? Might students think that all CP&P information was available via electronic means and not avail themselves of such resources as the 2,000 volume career library or the practice interview sessions? With a strong commitment to customer service, ease of use by clients and satisfying customer needs were both essential concerns. Our goals for providing information electronically were refined, and became the goals of providing (1) leads to information, services, and resources available through CP&P in other formats and settings and (2) substantive stand-alone information also available at the office itself. Thus, the form to request a reference letter from a professor, the library acquisitions list (retitled "New Books") or the list of program titles and times might be available in full-text format, while a discussion of considerations in writing a personal statement for law school would not. Instead, the student interested in law school would be directed through the gopher to programs, advising, and resources available in the office that relate to the law school application process.

In preparation for developing this gopher, the librarian, along with other team members, first researched career information on the Internet. The primary purpose was to explore similar career center gophers at other locations. Few such gophers exist, and their arrangement and resources varied greatly. The team also conducted some preliminary searching of Internet resources related to career issues and employment. These resources were found to be diffuse, inconsistent, and often discovered only serendipitously, making them especially difficult for the casual user of the Internet. More experienced Internet users could use a guide such as Riley's "Employment Opportunities and Job Resources."[3] In fact, a recent CP&P project done in conjunction with the University of Michigan School of Information and Library Studies to address the problem resulted in "Job Search and Employment Opportunities: Best Bets on the Net," a subject oriented resource guide to job search and employment.[4] The ease of searching college and university gopher sites for career center gophers varied widely. Some were clearly pathed through "Student Affairs" or "Student Services" folders. Others were found in such creatively titled folders as "Opportunity Knocks." The arrangement and content of the gophers also differed. These ranged from a single document detailing all staff and services of the career center, to clearly delineated folders for recruiting, programs, etc., to extensive referral directories. Finally, other gopher sites at the University of Michigan were explored.

This process of "surfing the Internet" provided a number of valuable starting assumptions. As we continued to access and use gophers across the country, we began to conceive of some of our technical requirements: the information needed to be easily accessed — neither all in a single file, nor buried so many levels deeply that students would abandon the search in frustration. We wanted clearly labeled folders and files, specific and useful information, and limited file length. It became clear that not only content, but technical details and arrangement, would impact the usability of the CP&P gopher.

CP&P then developed an internal cross-functional team to create the CP&P gopher. The task force reported directly to the Director of the office, who was a team member for the early months only. An important consideration as the team embarked on a long-term project to develop a CP&P gopher was maintaining staff investment and interest in the gopher. Ownership of the gopher by all staff was an explicitly stated outcome of the task force. Involvement on the part of all staff is important not only to make certain that the gopher is fully utilized and included in referrals by staff, but also to ensure that contributions to the gopher information are updated and expanded by all staff. In order to achieve this office-wide commitment, the task force worked through existing structures to involve staff. Once the preliminary research of Internet resources yielded several other career center gophers, other professional staff were taught how to use the gopher to access such information and were encouraged to explore these other gophers.

STRUCTURING THE CP&P GOPHER

With the foundation principles in place, the difficult task of structuring the gopher began. The challenge of the task force was to arrange the required information logically, in a consistent manner, and with easy access for end users in mind. The abundance of information to be included covered such diverse topics as a list of programs by date; suggestions for requesting reference letters from faculty, descriptions of such services as counseling and walk-in advising, job search information, and "hot tips" and resource information. The task force faced fundamental questions about how career information is or should be arranged. These questions included:

- What are the logical groupings of career information?
- Should the "professional" language of the career field be used, or the "natural" language in which questions are often asked?
- How could information be made easily available (without searching through several layers) while still maintaining a logical organization?

The arrangement of a gopher is by necessity linear and hierarchical, yet the information contained in this gopher was not linear, but interconnected. Reflecting this complexity while adhering to an internal logic led the task force to wrestle with large abstract concepts while simultaneously considering the individual details regarding information provision. For example, the information about a job search could be presented in numerous organizational schemes. The information could be progressive: resume, cover letter, researching employers, and so forth. Or, informational segments could be generated and arranged alphabetically, e.g., cover letter, researching employers, resume, since the computer screen would display these files as a list. The information could also be arranged not by the type of information, but by the status of the user, whether a first year student, graduate student, preprofessional student, etc. Would students identify most with their need or their classification? While these are questions that come to the fore in many ways when any informational materials are designed, the electronic format seemed to intensify the importance of these determinations. The linear approach of the gopher precludes browsing as through a book. The concerns that librarians have articulated about the browsing limitations of online catalogs as compared to card catalogs were reflected to some extent in considerations regarding the gopher format. It became important that both the conceptualization and the visual format of the arrangement be ones that users could navigate easily.

The use of a TQM tool called the affinity diagram assisted in the sorting and resorting of information. Each discrete body of information (typically equal to one document file on the gopher server) was written on a single slip of paper. These notes were then physically grouped by affinity, arranged and rearranged, subsumed within larger headings or folded into other groups. The inductive reasoning behind this exercise proved challenging for some in the task force. It demanded that preconceived groupings of activities, concepts and information be abandoned in order to redefine an organization appropriate to an electronic format. At times, the internal structure of the services of the office itself was discarded for a logic that more closely reflected the way in which users would typically access information. Using the experience of the librarian and the career development expert, in particular, a system that reflected the natural query patterns of users was developed.

Even at the highest level of our gopher—the main menu that would list each general category as a folder—the task force was faced with decisions regarding arrangement. While a straightforward alphabetical approach was at first considered, the menu was instead carefully arranged to reflect potential use by students. Introductions came first, general information followed, and specific aspects (such as reference letter information) came last. In order to accommodate students in their self-definitions and to help them navigate the gopher, a section on "How to Get Started" was included which provided overviews designed for students at different academic levels.

The language of the gopher was another consideration that illustrated the similarity between gopher design and publication design. Like all professions, the career development area has its own jargon: experiential learning rather than internships, self-assessment tools rather than career tests, and so forth. The career professionals were open to examining this language in relation to end-user convenience. Because the gopher is likely to be used off-site, the luxury of further clarification of terms is not available. The stated goal of the gopher—24 hour access to an office without walls—could by its nature inhibit the transfer of information if not designed effectively. To the greatest extent possible, the task force attempted to name folders and files with "user" language that would facilitate access to pertinent information in an efficient manner.

The task force agreed that succinct information was the preferred level of detail for making the gopher user-friendly. Still, there remained a strong desire to provide complete information. As information professionals know, providing incomplete and potentially incorrect information is actually a disservice to clients. Furthermore, the electronic format of the gopher limits arrangement to an outline-type of embedded informational search. Anyone who has used a gopher product knows the frustration of tunneling through several layers of files only to discover that the information being sought is unavailable or is less than expected. The task force therefore attempted to eliminate lengthy sessions of going from screen to screen for leads to information and resources. The goal was to balance the need to provide high quality complete information with the desire to provide information that was immediately helpful.

After the task force had agreed on basic principles of arrangement for the gopher, a prototype was unveiled to staff for their input. The staff worked together to discuss content and arrangement of the gopher as outlined by the task force. This proved to be an important step in conceptualizing the final product. Professional staff had strong feelings, based in theoretical constructs, that determined preferences for informational arrangement. Extensive notes were taken on staff discussion which were used by the task force in reformulating and refining the gopher outline. For example, the staff struggled with the area of job searching. Should all programs, systems, and job fairs focusing on permanent employment be separated from those regarding part time or internship opportunities? Or, should students be able to access the information on all career conferences together, regardless of the type of opportunities represented in them? Professional staff preferences combined with personal experiences regarding the ways in which users were currently requesting such information determined that the arrangement would focus first on the type of job search (e.g. permanent vs. experiential).

The University of Michigan is one of the largest feeder institutions to professional and graduate schools in the nation; therefore the section on advanced education was of equal importance to employment issues. Staff were presented with two distinct models. The first arranged graduate education by the type of program (e.g., law school, medical school, professional schools, academic graduate programs); each "interest area" was further subdivided into topics such as admissions information and testing, investigating schools, personal statements, etc. The second model was arranged first by the content: personal statements, timelines, admissions tests, etc., with each of those categories further subdivided by type of program (e.g., admissions tests–medical school, admissions tests–law school). As staff wrestled with these alternative and equally logical arrangements, it became clear that based on the way that users typically present their questions regarding these topics the first model was more reflective of the way that clients would actually use the gopher. This feedback loop was continued throughout the design process. In some cases, all professional staff were involved in looking at arrangements. In other cases, the staff member responsible for a functional area met with the gopher task force to discuss a particular portion of the gopher structure.

In addition to involving staff for increased investment, the gopher had to be coordinated with other office technologies, those established as well as those being developed. For example, the office was simultaneously inaugurating an online recruiting system. A primary goal of this system was to expand student understanding of recruiting to include not simply on-campus interviews, but also leads to and networks of employers off campus. The systems therefore needed to be complementary. It was important to establish M-LINE (Leads to Interviews, Networks and Employers, CP&P's online recruiting system) as the first choice location of information concerning employer networks. The gopher needed to have strong referral links in order to channel students interested in recruiting toward direct access to the M-LINE system. Short and long term goals sometimes differed. For example, direct hypertextual links between the gopher and other technologies were a long term consideration. The office commitment to increased use of technology indicates that such links will be considerations in the development or choice of additional technologies.

IMPLEMENTATION

Implementation of the gopher clearly needed to be multiphasic to be manageable. Those documents that could be directly uploaded and were appropriate for electronic formats were ready to be added to this new informational product, allowing the task force to begin mounting the gopher while continuing the design process itself. The goal of mounting the gopher was realized in September 1994, 7 months after the task force was originally charged. The first stage of implementation concentrated on essentials: information about office hours, location and the like, combined with readily accessible files on programs and resources. The initial structure became as follows:

> Welcome to CP&P
> About CP&P
> CP&P Hours and Location
> Our Staff
> CP&P Mission
> CP&P Calendar of Events
> How Students Can Use CP&P (separate files by class level)

CP&P Handouts
New Books in the CP&P Library

Technical details became important at the implementation stage. The University's Information Technology Division has established conventions for the GOpher BLUE server that CP&P needed to follow. Again, the task force found themselves reviewing the logic of the arrangement and the potential end user approach to the design. For example, each folder could be titled with 32 characters only; thus, folders with carefully written titles such as "How Students and Alumni/ae Can Use CP&P" had to be renamed. Such conventions proved challenging in an office that carefully crafts titles, publicity, and other written materials. In addition, the gopher software did not support text formatting with underlined, bold, or italic characters. Only upper and lower case, tabs, and spaces were available for use in formatting information, increasing readability, or organizing information. "About" files (which explain the purpose and contents of that level in the gopher tree, provide contact information and an updating schedule) needed to be created for each new level in the gopher, and again were based on conventions put forth by the University. Keeping customer service considerations in mind, the task force carefully designed both titles and text to conform to these conventions.

Implementation also meant that there had to be a committment to maintaining the currency and accuracy of the information. The task force returned to the goal of staff ownership, which included ownership of the content of the product itself. Bringing up a new and exciting system provides an energy that helps to keep staff invested; now it became important to plan for the ongoing maintenance along with continuous improvement. Establishing a systematic model for keeping the gopher viable over time was from the first an essential component to the task force's charge. A difficult question was whether gopher updates should be the responsibility of individual staff members, of an ongoing gopher committee, or of the technical services unit of the office. Because the gopher files had to be created in such a specific format, it was decided early on that all uploads would be done through the technical services area; however there was ambivalence concerning the creation of new files, and the responsibility for providing updates. The task force decided that during the implementation phases, it would become a standing committee and would assume responsibility for updates along with the mounting of new folders and files. The task force was redesignated as a committee cochaired by the librarian and the systems analyst. It was also recommended that the committee should have staggered rotating membership, providing for both stability and ongoing investment by all professional staff.

One of the initial tasks of this committee will be to develop an ongoing system for gopher maintenance. First, the committee will survey other staff to determine what information already exists in printed form that will be inserted into the outline of the gopher. Information that exists but not in an appropriate format will next be revised for inclusion. Finally, new information that is not already gathered in a printed format or in a combination that reflects the gopher arrangement and these gopher files will need to be created. There are several options under consideration concerning the staffing of the committee and the organization of its workflow. The committee may be staffed by someone who has the responsibility for creating files, e.g., an intern from the School of Information and Library Studies or from a College Student Personnel Program, or a student staff member with a writing background. Alternatively, individual office staff could prepare documents specifically for the gopher. Newly created documents, however, may need editing or approval. The responsibility for developing a system for consistent updating of materials may also be configured in any number of ways. The committee could provide updates to all files, or staff may have responsibility for maintaining the gopher as a part of ongoing publicity efforts already underway. As the year progresses, the gopher committee will be addressing these maintenance issues while continuing to phase in new gopher information.

Ongoing evaluation as well as ongoing development will also be a focus of the committee. The gopher, by its very nature, is a flexible and easily modifiable means of providing information. The structure as well as the content may be updated reflecting changes in office services or client needs. The staff ownership of this product will provide a continuous feedback loop from the professional side. On the student side, feedback is sought both through the system itself and through other mechanisms. The final gopher structure includes a "How are We Doing?" folder giving users a way to offer suggestions and comments. In addition, CP&P has in recent years increased the use of student focus groups in order to more effectively encourage and channel student feedback. Focus groups now forming to respond to CP&P's informational services will provide a means for receiving concrete information about how students use the gopher service.

The demand for career information, already enormous, has increased along with the information explosion. Our gopher site, after only 3 months, outnumbered many established sections of GOpher BLUE, with 2396 "hits" or individual user access interactions. The CP&P Gopher was mounted on September 8, 1994. The office promoted the system in-house through a bulletin board display and references to the gopher in mailings and other information and publicity. The gopher is located in the section of GOpher BLUE called "The University and Ann Arbor," along with gophers provided by schools, colleges, individual departments, and files about happenings in town and local restaurants (see Figure 1 for the gopher's structural outline).

CONCLUSION

A process first seen as transferring our current information products to a new format actually presented CP&P with a variety of considerations regarding the provision of career information. Its foundation principles of embracing technological means in order to provide services and of working towards the goal of an office without walls allowed it to review much of the user/information interface in the office. The process of designing the gopher reflected the intellectual and discovery processes that our users must undertake as they explore career issues and information. The new formats which were planned did indeed impact the way in which information is presented and received. For career information providers and users, technological enhancements will need to be viewed and designed with this understanding. In order to serve our clients, there will be an increasing need to revisit arrangements, patterns of delivery, and expectations for use.

```
                        FIGURE 1

Structural Outline
Career Planning & Placement Gopher
University of Michigan

About CP&P File                  Job Search Strategies
                                   Internships & Summer Jobs
Overview of CP&P                       Summer Postings
  Hours & Location                     Public Service Internship Program
  Our Staff                            Conferences through CP&P
  Overview of Services                 Resume Express
  Mission                              M-Line online recruitment
  Whom do we Serve                     Counseling & Advising through CP&P
                                   Permanent
How to Use CP&P                        M-Line online recruitment
  First Year Students                  Job Bulletin
  Second Year Students                 Resume Express
  Third Year Students                  Conferences through CP&P
  Fourth and Fifth Year Students       Library Resources
  Graduate Students                    Counseling & Advising through CP&P
  Students of Color
  Students with Disabilities     Graduate and Professional School
  Preprofessional Students         Academic Graduate Programs
  International Students               Deciding to Go
  Alumni                               Investigating Schools
  Faculty/Staff                        Personal Statements
                                       Letters of Reference
Calendar of Events                     Admissions Tests
                                   Law
Resources                            (same set of subheadings)
  CP&P Handouts                   Medicine
  CP&P Library                       (same set of subheadings)
  New Books at CP&P               Business
                                     (same set of subheadings)
Career Planning/Decision Making  Other Professional Schools
  Career Decision Making             (same set of subheadings)
    Career Tests & Assessment
    Choosing a Major             Reference Letter File Center
    Choosing Careers               Opening a File
    Counseling & Advising at CP&P   Sending Letters
  Career Exploration               Checking on your File
    Networking on Campus           How to Update Files
    Informational Interviewing     FAQs
    "Career Pathways" programs     For Faculty/Letter Writers
    Outreach Programs
    Counseling & Advising at CP&P How Are We Doing'?
                                     Comment Box
                                     Email address for questions
```

REFERENCES

1. University of Michigan. Division of Student Affairs. Career Planning and Placement Office. *Strategic Plan.* Ann Arbor, MI: University of Michigan, 1992 [mimeo], p.7.

2. University of Michigan. Division of Student Affairs. Career Planning and Placement Office. *CAS Self Assessment.* Ann Arbor, MI: University of Michigan, 1994 [mimeo], n.p.

3. Riley, M. *Employment Opportunities and Job Resources. http://www.jobtrack. com/jobguide*

4. Ray, Philip and Bradley Taylor. *Job Search and Employment Opportunities: Best Bets from the Net.* Version 1.2, Dec. 1994. gopher//una.hh.lib.unich.edu/00/ inetdirsstacks/employment%3araytay. HTML version available through http://asa. ugl.lib.umich.edu/chdocs/employment/job-guide.toc/html

V. ACCESS ISSUES

Job Searching on the Internet:
A Public Library Perspective

Rebecca Berkowitz
Heather Brodie

SUMMARY. The Internet is a technology that is opening vast new doors to public librarians and patrons. Enhanced service to job hunters is one of these new doors. There are many resources on the Internet of potential use to job seekers as well as sophisticated tools for finding these resources. Offering access to job searching on the Internet will require a great deal of equipment, planning, preparation and expertise. This paper will examine the possibilities and practicalities for the public library. *[Article copies available from The Haworth Document Delivery Service: 1-800-342-9678. E-mail address: getinfo@haworth.com]*

Rebecca Berkowitz is Reference Librarian, Legal Bibliographer and Internet Coordinator, and Heather Brodie is Reference Librarian, Interlibrary Loan Officer and Head of Commercial Services, at the Framingham Public Library, 49 Lexington Street, Framingham, MA 01701.

[Haworth co-indexing entry note]: "Job Searching on the Internet: A Public Library Perspective." Berkowitz, Rebecca and Heather Brodie. Co-published simultaneously in *The Reference Librarian* (The Haworth Press, Inc.) No. 55, 1996, pp. 99-105; and: *Career Planning and Job Searching in the Information Age* (ed: Elizabeth A. Lorenzen) The Haworth Press, Inc., 1996, pp. 99-105. Single or multiple copies of this article are available from The Haworth Document Delivery Service [1-800-342-9678, 9:00 a.m. - 5:00 p.m. (EST). E-mail address: getinfo@haworth.com].

INTRODUCTION

Experience has shown that exploring databases on the Internet is time consuming. At this point in time, the Internet by its very nature is not a reliable, predictable, consistent resource. Therefore, it is important to have realistic expectations regarding its ability to consistently deliver information. Public library service must meet the needs of a diverse clientele who are generally seeking an immediate response. The issues of access, space, equipment, funding and expertise immediately come to mind.

The Framingham Public Library is a medium sized library serving a heterogeneous town of sixty-five thousand people approximately twenty-five miles west of Boston, Massachusetts. The town is surrounded by smaller bedroom communities who have come to depend on Framingham's larger collection. The library is a member of the thirty member Minuteman Library Network which provides a common catalog and other technical services, including Internet access. In determining how best to meet the information needs of this community regarding its access to the Internet, reference librarians at the Framingham Public Library explored the issues of access, training and customer service. The purpose of this paper is to explore some of these unique issues confronting public librarians who are attempting to assist patrons using the Internet to support their job search.

ACCESS AND RESOURCES

Means of access is a major factor in determining the viability of Internet use for job searching. Hardware, software, and type of connection will determine patrons' access to resources and navigation tools. Although many interfaces are similar, there are different protocols and users must learn each one if they intend to telnet to databases. Furthermore, logins at remote hosts can be limited to a small number of users, for a limited amount of time.

Public gophers can be used to avoid some of the problems of telnet but they too will often have unique protocols, may limit the number of users and the time a guest is allowed to use a port. Traveling via public gophers is often slow.

Gopher clients eliminate most of these problems and allow the user to create bookmarks to easily return to favorite sources, cut down on response time and generally facilitate travel. Any serious user of the Internet will eventually want to use an on-site gopher client. However, this is a big undertaking for a public library and probably will only be possible for libraries in larger systems or networks where greater funding is available.

The World Wide Web is currently one of the most popular applications on the Internet. The sound effects and graphics have taken the public by storm. With access to the proper search tools, the WWW provides many of the advantages of Gophers and then some. However, full use of the Web requires specific hardware needs.

Any serious user of the Internet will need a personal computer with sufficient memory to handle the large documents that can be found on the Net. It opens up possibilities that the use of "dumb" terminals preclude. Speedy printers with sizable buffer zones are also required. Paper, inkjets, virus free floppy disks will be necessary. Publicly funded institutions that are often struggling to maintain level funding for their book budgets must now find funding to provide access to the information superhighway.

Space and equipment must be considered. Hardware takes up space. Unless the library has a local area network, terminals or microcomputers must be dedicated to Internet usage. They cannot then be used to search the catalog or magazine indexes which is, after all, the mainstay of the public library. If extra hardware is not available, some mechanism must be developed to allocate terminals and ensure the availability of the catalog.

TRAINING ISSUES

Some staff assistance will be required for patrons using the Internet for the job search. Some patrons will require a great deal of assistance. Are staff available? Are they trained? Are other services being reduced and if so is that the intent?

Experience has shown that training staff to navigate the Internet is a time consuming prospect. As the use of the Internet has grown, professionals have acquired different levels of interest and expertise, which will probably lead to some staff specialization. At the present time there is some concern about providing uneven service to patrons at the Framingham Public Library. At the present time there is not a clear plan in place that corrects this situation, but settling this training issue will indeed take time as the technology continues to change and grow.

Patrons' expectations must be carefully considered. Libraries in Massachusetts are funded and governed primarily on the local level and are answerable directly to local voters. The mission statement of most public libraries includes the concept of meeting the information requirements of the community. Media reports on the information superhighway have probably led some people to believe that everything is available on the Internet and easily accessed, which is simply not true. Job databases on the Internet fill a gap for some libraries in some areas, but are not always useful for all patrons. The needs of many job seekers looking for local jobs may still best be served using conventional library resources. Local employment opportunities for many communities are currently not well covered on the Internet.

Anyone with any experience on the Internet knows that it can be sluggish. Things change daily. A database accessed yesterday may be closed today for no apparent reason. Sometimes the book marks refuse to appear, gophers will not open, Veronica is unavailable, there are not enough incoming ports to accommodate guests trying to access a node. A search can be very time consuming. Public libraries cannot guarantee much once a patron has accessed the Internet, and educating patrons concerning these constraints presents a challenge to public librarians.

POSSIBILITIES FOR SERVICE

What services could/should a public library effectively provide? Public libraries have long considered assisting job seekers an important and desirable function. Many patrons looking for a job come to the reference desk for assistance. They can be divided into categories and doing so helps evaluate the potential effectiveness of using the Internet in order to help them meet their information needs.

The first category of job seeker is looking for job listings. Framingham Public Library currently offers largely local job listings. National information is limited to large directories of short profiles, stock reports and magazine articles. Patrons searching farther afield than Massachusetts for jobs seek assistance from other providers, but they are probably the group who could most benefit from job searching on the Internet. *The Internet Yellow Pages* devotes three pages to job listings. Federal jobs and other specialized categories are heavily represented in national databases. One of the major databases for federal employment opportunities is Fedjobs; it is compiled by the Office of Personnel Management. The Online Career Center offers job openings as well as resume postings and information on a limited number of companies. The database is easy to search and is accessible both by Gopher and through the Web. MedSearch America is another national database. It is easy to search by location, job category or keyword. The "Chronicle of Higher Education" has put the equivalent of its print job openings on the Internet. These opportunities are in academia nationwide. Searching can be limited by geographic area and field. Many gophers include job listings on their main menus, including the Minuteman Library gopher (mln.lib. ma.us). In order to make these services widely known throughout a community, extensive publicity is needed. Such a major commitment must be examined within the context of the strategic and long range plans of this or any other institution. The second category of job seeker is looking for information about particular companies or industries. The Internet offers access to commercial services that provide this type of current information. Additionally, the Internet provides access to a variety of databases with extensive business information. For example, one notable source is the Department of Commerce's National Trade Data Bank. This is an attractive possibility for public library service because of community needs for access to business resources.

A third category is looking for vocational guidance. Included here are people coming to the library looking for information on interviewing, resume and cover letter writing, writing business plans and starting businesses as well as those exploring different career options. Even though there are many print sources that are quite good, some of these are now being made available on the

Internet from the United States government. Resources such as the Occupational Outlook Handbook provide a good example.

CONCLUSION

The Internet has some exciting possibilities. It is fast becoming a valuable resource for any information agency. However, from the point of view of the public reference librarian, the Internet is just another tool, and like any other tool it has its shortcomings. One concern lies in the lack of attribution on the Internet. It is sometimes impossible to determine the source of the information on some databases and therefore its accuracy and timeliness. Another concern is the issue of copyright compliance, and plagiarism. Any public library considering offering public access to the Internet for job searching should proceed with great caution. Public libraries should choose carefully what services they can offer and then do an excellent job providing those services. Providing access to the Internet for job hunting does not have to be a yes or no proposition. An organization could try providing limited services based on their particular situation. It could be limited in time of day or week. Certain data bases could be pre-selected, and terminals set aside. Dedicated staffing could support patrons if only a few data bases were used and not all the time. This has many advantages.

The Framingham Public Library will be offering public access to the Internet through the Minuteman Library Network gopher. Job search resources are a menu item on the gopher. Staff assistance will be available to patrons. The service will be actively promoted, but steps are being taken to ensure that other services do not suffer. For example, not all terminals will provide access to the Internet so that the library's online catalog and periodical databases will always be available. Patrons will continue to be encouraged to use a variety of sources for all of their information needs.

Any decision about providing Internet services must be preceded by some corporate soul searching and extensive planning, while considering the following questions:

- Do you have the equipment and space? Can you afford it?
- Do you have the staff? Do they have the expertise? If not, what plans are there for training?

- Is this part of your mission?
- What are your goals and objectives in offering this service?
- Are they consistent with the overall goals and objectives of the institution? Can the results be evaluated?
- How will you be enhancing the services you are currently offering to job seekers? Are they looking for such services?

A Look at Internet Privacy
and Security Issues and Their Relationship
to the Electronic Job Search:
Implications for Librarians
and Career Services Professionals

Greg Iaccarino

SUMMARY. As more job searchers use the Internet and on-line services, librarians and career services professionals will play a greater role in educating clients about the ethical implications of an electronic job search. In this study, "electronic privacy" will be defined, and laws which govern electronic security as well as reactions to those laws will be reviewed. Corporate policies on employee electronic accounts will be discussed. Technological methods being used to ensure confidentiality and privacy will be examined, and the role and responsibility of career services professionals and librarians in training clients on an ethical job search will be addressed. *[Article copies available from The Haworth Document Delivery Service: 1-800-342-9678. E-mail address: getinfo@haworth.com]*

Greg Iaccarino is Academic Advisor, Eastern Illinois University. He is an active member of the American College Personnel Association, National Association of Student Personnel Administrators and the National Academic Advising Association.

The author is indebted to Elizabeth Lorenzen and Patricia Peterson for their technological support and assistance.

[Haworth co-indexing entry note]: "A Look at Internet Privacy and Security Issues and Their Relationship to the Electronic Job Search: Implications for Librarians and Career Services Professionals." Iaccarino, Greg. Co-published simultaneously in *The Reference Librarian* (The Haworth Press, Inc.) No. 55, 1996, pp. 107-113; and: *Career Planning and Job Searching in the Information Age* (ed: Elizabeth A. Lorenzen) The Haworth Press, Inc., 1996, pp. 107-113. Single or multiple copies of this article are available from The Haworth Document Delivery Service [1-800-342-9678, 9:00 a.m. - 5:00 p.m. (EST). E-mail address: getinfo@haworth.com].

107

INTRODUCTION

As more electronic job searchers use the Internet and on-line services, librarians and career services professionals will play a greater role and responsibility in educating their clients about the ethical implications of an electronic job search. Unlike the U.S. mail system, in which an applicant uses a sealed envelope to send credentials to an employer, the Internet is not as secure. Job seekers posting their credentials to on-line services do not know who is reading them. In most cases, on-line users need a password to access their accounts. However, even a password does not prevent unauthorized individuals from entering computer networks. Many employers also claim that they have a legal right to access employees files on company-owned computer networks. These and other issues will influence how librarians and career services professionals conduct electronic job search workshops for their clients. The purpose of this article is to give an overview of some of the ethical, privacy and security issues of an electronic job search and to discuss the role and responsibility of professionals in educating clients about these issues.

ETHICAL, PRIVACY AND SECURITY ISSUES OF AN ELECTRONIC JOB SEARCH

Electronic Privacy Defined

According to Rotenberg (1993), three characteristics of "privacy" are: *confidentiality* (communication between two sources without interference by a third source), *anonymity* (the act of sending a message without identifying oneself) and *data protection* (keeping data from access by unauthorized parties). Witt (1992) defined the right-to-privacy as "Intrusion upon another's seclusion, appropriation of another's name or likeness, unreasonable publicity of another's private life, and publicity that unreasonably places the other in a false light before the public" (p. 547).

Electronic Privacy Court Cases and Legislation

The issue of electronic privacy has been debated for almost 30 years in the courts and recently in Congress. In *Katz v. United States* in 1967, the United States Supreme Court found unconstitutional the Federal Government's attachment of listening and recording devices in public phone booths without a caller's consent or a court order (Wintersheimer, 1988). Though *Katz* was effective for telephone users, neither it nor subsequent laws in the 1970s and early 1980s covered the rapidly expanding Internet and on-line electronic communication services. These laws, according to the Office of Technology Assessment (a Congressional group): "were largely developed for a time when telegraphs, typewriters and mimeographs were the commonly used office technologies and business was conducted by paper documents sent by mail" (Maize, 1994, p. new09230013). As a result, Congress in 1986 passed the *Electronic Communications Privacy Act (ECPA)*.

The ECPA is the first major legislation to cover electronic communication on the Internet. The Act ensures "privacy protection against both interception of electronic communications while in transaction and unauthorized intrusion into electronic communication stored on a system" (Hernandez, 1988, p. 29). An outside party can only access a user's account by a court order in a legal investigation. The user must be notified 14 days before the account files are searched. If these terms are broken, the violator can be fined $250.00 for each infraction up to a maximum of $10,000 plus any damages suffered by the user.

In a business environment, ECPA is in effect when a person unaffiliated with the company illegally surveys an employee's files. However, the act does NOT apply when an internal company supervisor accesses staff accounts for business purposes, such as for a company memo. More importantly, ECPA only covers public government employers, not private ones (Casarez, 1992). Private employees cite this lack of coverage as one of the Act's major drawbacks (Hernandez, 1988). As a result of these drawbacks, the electronic job searcher cannot be assured of complete confidentiality while conducting a search from the private employer's computer. The employee faces the risk of sanctions or some other form of reprimand if the supervisor discovers, while surveying files, a confidential job search.

In an attempt to question ECPA's drawbacks, Senator Paul Simon (D-IL) introduced the *Privacy for Consumers and Workers Act*

(PCWA). Under the Act, private employers would be required to give advance notice to their staffs before reading files. Examples of "advance notice" include beeper sounds or a message at the log-in screen. Employers would also have to "beep" the user if they wanted to monitor the account while the user was simultaneously on it. In addition, employers would have to review their electronic monitoring policies during candidate interviews (Cappel, 1993). As a result of this Act, the electronic job searcher's confidentiality would be increased.

Corporate and Educational Responses to ECPA and PCWA

In response to ECPA and PCWA, corporations are contending that they have the legal right to monitor the activities of their computer networks. A number of organizations, including United Parcel Service, FedEx, General Motors, McDonnell Douglas, Warner Brothers, Citibank, Eastman Kodak, Pacific Bell, Nordstrom and Bank of Boston, have posted messages on staff login screens about the right to access files (Cappel, 1993). Nordstrom's statement is reprinted below:

> E-mail is a company resource and is provided as a business communications tool. Employees with legitimate business purposes may have the need to view your e-mail messages. It is also possible that others may view your messages inadvertently, since there is no guarantee of privacy for e-mail messages. Please use your good judgment as you use the e-mail system. (Cappel, 1993, p. 6)

Colleges and universities are also establishing policies for their computer networks. At the University of Delaware, for example, new students desiring user accounts must pass the University's new "Electronic Community Citizenship" examination to show that they understand the regulations and ethics of electronic communication (*Chronicle,* 1994). The multiple choice test consists of ten questions randomly selected from ten different categories and includes such topics as password security, recognizing copyright restrictions on software, and penalties for deliberate misuse of computer access.

ROLE AND RESPONSIBILITY OF ELECTRONIC JOB SEARCH TRAINERS

As security and privacy issues become more relevant in the electronic job search, librarians and career services professionals should define their roles and responsibilities in informing their clients about these issues in electronic job search workshops. During the workshops, clients should be warned that thousands of individuals can view their resumes and applications on on-line services (unlike the traditional U.S. Mail letter which is only viewed by the recipient). Trainers should inform clients about computer hackers or other unauthorized individuals who can break into confidential files and accounts. If a break-in occurs, confidential information such as address, telephone number and past job history can be in an unauthorized person's hands. The hacker could freely forward this information via e-mail or file transfer protocol (ftp) to other people without the client's knowledge. The computer hacker could also intercept a resume or cover letter which must reach the employer by a certain deadline. Unauthorized access could also result in a computer virus which would damage important job search credentials. As a result of these risks, one of the most important responsibilities of trainers is to educate clients about technological methods of keeping a file secure. Some examples of these methods are *Password, Encryption* and *Firewalls.*

The *password* is a secret number or phrase known only to the electronic job searcher. It should be "at least six characters long, have a mixture of uppercase, lowercase and numbers, is not a word, and is not a set of adjacent keyboard keys" (Krol, 1992, p. 40). Names should never be used as passwords because computer hackers usually use them to break into accounts.

In *encryption,* job searchers substitute the regular print of their resumes with other letters and numbers which cannot be read by unauthorized parties. The credentials are sent via a "public key" as an encrypted message to the employer. The interviewer then uses the "private key" to decrypt (decode) the message into regular text. The public key *cannot* be used to decrypt the message. Since the job seeker and the interviewer are the only people who have the private key code, no one will know the confidential information of a resume nor other credential. Encryption systems available for demonstration include Lotus CC and Microsoft Mail, Privacy Enhanced Mail (PEM) and Pretty Good Privacy (PGP) (Wallich, 1993).

The most advanced security method, which is becoming the main form of protection, is *firewalls.* There are many types of firewalls, but basically what they all do is create a connection between a network and the Internet that can restrict both ingoing and outgoing information. For more information about this security technique, consult Steven Bellovin and William Cheswick's *Firewalls and Internet Security: Repelling the Wily Hacker* (Bernstein, 1994).

In addition to the preceding protective methods, trainers should also be aware of the *Computer Emergency Response Team (CERT)*, an organization which oversees and investigates the activities of computer hackers in cooperation with the Federal Bureau of Investigation (Panettieri, 1994). Its address is: CERT Coordination Center, Software Engineering Institute, Carnegie Mellon University, Pittsburgh, PA 15213-3890. CERT's 24 hour telephone number is (412) 268-7090 and its e-mail address is: CERT@CERT.SEI.CMU.EDU.

Due to the increase in the number of corporate e-mail policies, Internet users should be warned regarding the ethical implications of performing an electronic job search from an office computer. Using the company's electronic hardware could be construed as being as unethical as using its stationery or telephone for personal use. Users should also be warned that as soon as a resume is posted in an electronic database on the Internet, they basically lose control over who can access their resume, so their privacy in regards to their current employer could be at stake.

FUTURE ISSUES: HOW RESPONSIBLE MUST AN ELECTRONIC TRAINER BE?

As more clients attend Internet workshops in the coming years, trainers will continue to have a role in educating clients about ethical issues in an electronic job search. Though providing the client with important information, is the service provider at risk if a recommended security technique does not work, thus resulting in problems for the client? Will clients in the future hold trainers liable for the advice given in workshops? A prediction here is that clients may put forth accusations if something goes wrong. In order to prepare for this possibility, trainers should develop a policy which does not make them liable in the event of a problem. If the trainer needs assistance in formulating a liability policy, he or she should contact appropriate legal counsel.

There will always be risks and ethical implications in using electronic job search services. The main reason behind these risks is the accessibility of confidential job search credentials in cyberspace. It is predicted that many more job searchers will use the Information Highway as a means to secure a position. The security of a sealed letter in the traditional mail can only be achieved if users continually stay updated on the latest security methods and use discretion as they access resources. As the Information superhighway's growth outpaces that of its current regulation, some final words of wisdom are: "Be careful, be skeptical, and don't assume anyone is not monitoring."

REFERENCES

Bernstein, D. (1994 October 1). Insulate against Internet intruders. *Datamation, 40* (19), 49-52.

Cappel, J.J. (1993, December). Closing the Email privacy gap (electronic monitoring of employees). *Journal of Systems Management, 44*, 6-11.

Casarez, N. (1992, Summer). Electronic mail and employee relations: why privacy must be considered. *Public Relations Quarterly, 37*, pp. 37-40.

Hernandez, R.H. (1988, November). ECPA and online computer privacy. *Federal Communications Law Journal, 41*, 17-41.

Krol, E. (1992). *The whole internet: Users guide and catalog.* Sebastopol, CA: O'Reilly & Associates, Inc.

Maize, K. (1994, September 23). Congressional group pushes computer privacy. *Newsbytes,* p. newo9230013.

New students at the University of Delaware have one extra test to take this year. (1994, October 19). *Chronicle of Higher Education, XLI*(9), p. A38.

Panettieri, J.C. (1994, November 28). Are your computers safe? *Information Week, n503,* pp. 34-48.

Panettieri, J.C. (1994, May 23). Guardian of the net. *Information Week, n476,* pp. 30-40.

Rotenberg, M. (1993, August). Communications privacy: Implications for network design. *Communications of the ACM, 36*, pp. 61-68.

Wintersheimer, L.A. (1988). Privacy vs. law enforcement—can the two be reconciled? *University of Cincinnati Law Review, 57*, 315-42.

APPENDICES

Internet Resources and Their URLs

This listing supplies the reader with URL's for all resources listed in this volume. They are cited alphabetically by the name of the resource.

Academe This Week	http://chronicle.merit.edu/.ads/.links.html
Academic Position Network	gopher://wcni.cis.umn.edu:11111/1
American Mathematical Society	http://e-math.ams.org/web/employ/employ.html
American Physician and Scientist (APS)	gopher://aps.acad-phy-sci.com/
ARL Gopher	gopher://arl.cni.org/
Art Job	http://www.webart.com/artjob
Brandeis University's Hiatt Career Development Center Home Page	http://www.brandeis.edu/hiatt/hiatt_home.html
Career Mosaic	http://www.careermosaic.com:80/cm/
Careers, Jobs, Employment	gopher://honor.uc.wlu.edu:1020/1%20%20%23hfj/cl
Careers Online	http://www.ideaf.com/jobs/pps.htm
Catapult (Leo Charette)	http://www.jobweb.org/catapult/catapult.html
Chicago Tribune Job Finder	http://www.chicago.tribune.com/career/
Clearinghouse for Subject-Oriented Internet Resource Guides	gopher://una.hh.lib.umich.edu/11/inetdirs http://www.lib.umich.edu/chhome.html

[Haworth co-indexing entry note]: "Internet Resources and Their URLs." Co-published simultaneously in *The Reference Librarian* (The Haworth Press, Inc.) No. 55, 1996, pp. 115-118; and: *Career Planning and Job Searching in the Information Age* (ed: Elizabeth A. Lorenzen) The Haworth Press, Inc., 1996, pp. 115-118. Single or multiple copies of this article are available from The Haworth Document Delivery Service [1-800-342-9678, 9:00 a.m. - 5:00 p.m. (EST). E-mail address: getinfo@haworth.com].

115

A Compendium of Women's Resources	http://www.mit.edu:8001/people/sorokin/women/index.html
Corporation for Public Broadcasting's Jobline	http://www.cpb.org/jobline/jobline.htm
Direct Marketing World Jobs Center	http://www.dmworld.com/
Directory of Electronic Journals, News-letters, and Academic Discussion Lists	gopher://arl.cni.org/11/scomm/edir
Employment Opportunities and Job Resources on the Internet (Margaret F. Riley)	http://www.jobtrack.com/jobguide
E-Span (Interactive Employment Network)	http://www.espan.com/:80/ telnet:Fjob.mail.opm.gov
Fed Jobs	http://www.fedworld.gov
Fedworld	telnet://fedworld.gov ftp://ftp.fedworld.gov/jobs direct dial access 703-321-8020, 8-N-1, ANSI/VT100 terminal emulation
Finding Library Jobs & Library Employment: Navigating the Electronic Web (Fenner)	gopher://una.hh.lib.umich.edu/00/inetdirsstacks/jobs%3afenner
Frogjobs	listproc@list.cren.net
Galaxy (EINet)	http://galaxy.einet.net/galaxy/community/workplace.html
Gopher-Jewels	http://galaxy.einet.net/GJ/index.html
H.E.A.R.T. (Career Connection's Online Interactive Employment Network)	http://www.career.com
How to Compose Veronica Queries	gopher://veronica.scs.unr.edu:70/00/veronica/how-to-query-Veronica
Hytel-L	listserv@kentvm (Bitnet) listserv@kentvm.edu (Internet)
*Hytelnet	http://library.usask.ca/hytelnet/
Indiana State University's Career Resources page	http://odin.indstate.edu/level1.dir/career.html
Industrial Outlook Handbook	gopher://umslvma.umsl.edu:70/11//library/govdocs/indpro
JCIS-L	listserv@clpgh.org
Job Net (Bruce Brewer, West Georgia College)	gopher:sum.cc.westga.edu http://sun.cc.westga.edu/~coop/
Job Opportunities for Economists (JOE)	gopher://vuinfo.vanderbilt.edu:70/11/employment/joe
Job Resource List, Texas A & M University	http://ageninfo.tamu.edu/jobs.html

Job Search & Employment Opportunities:
  Best Bets From the Net
    (Phil Ray and Bradley Taylor)   http://asa.ugl.lib.umich.edu/chdocs/
                                             employment/job-guide.toc/html
                                             gopher://una.hh.lib.umich.edu/00/
                                             inetdirsstacks/employment%3araytay
Job Web   http://www.jobweb.com/
JobPlace   listserv@news.jobweb.org
JobPlace Home Page   http://news.jobweb.org/cgi-bin/lwgate/
                                             JOBPLACE/

Jobs, Employment, Placement Services and
Programs (D. Kovacs)   gopher://una.hh.lib.umich.edu:
                                             70/00/inetdirsstacks/acadlist.jobs
LC Marvel   gopher://marvel.loc.gov//employee/
                                             employ/

Librarian's Joblist - University of Illinois
  at Urbana-Champaign/GLIS   telnet://alexia.lis.uiuc.edu
                                             login = jobsrch, password = workfare
List of All Active Newsgroups   ftp://ftp.uu.net/usenet/news.answers/
                                             active-newsgroups/part1.2andpart2.2
List of Listservs (N. Carolina State)   gopher://dewey.lib.ncsu.edu:70/11/
                                             library/stacks/acadlist
Liszt of Email Discussion Lists   http://www.liszt.com
Lycos   http://lycos.cs.cmu.edu/
Medsearch America   http://www.medsearch.com/
Monster Board   gopher://gopher.medsearch.com:9001/
                                             http://www.monster.com:80/
NCSA Meta - Index   http://www.ncsa.uiuc.edu/SDG/
                                             Software/Mosaic/MetaIndex.html
Net-Happenings   majordomo@is.internic.net
                                             http://www.mid.net/NET/
                                             gopher://gopher.mid.net:7000/
New Jour   majordomo@ccat.sas.upenn.edu
New List   listserv@ndsuvml (Bitnet)
                                             listserv@vml.nodak.edu (Internet)
1993 State Industry Profiles   gopher://umslva.umsl.edu:70/11//
                                             library/govdocs/states
1993 U.S. Industry Profiles   gopher://umslva.umsl.edu:70/11//
                                             library/govdocs/indpro
Occupational Outlook Handbook   gopher://umslva.umslva.edu:70/11//
                                             library/govdocs/ooha/oohb
Online Career Center   http://www.occ.com/occ/
Riceinfo   gopher://riceinfo.rice.edu:70/11/Subject/
                                             Jobs
San Francisco Examiner Classifieds   http://sfgate.com/classifieds/index.html

San Jose Mercury Sun	http://www.sjmercury.com/class/
SPIE Online Employment Service	http://www.spie.org/web/employment/ employ_home.html
University of Illinois Urbana-Champaign's *Career Planning & Professional* *Development page*	http://www.cso.uiuc.edu/careers/ careers.top.html
Usenet Newsgroups *List of All Usenet Newsgroups*	ftp://ftp.uu.net/networking/news/ config/newsgroups.Z
ba.jobs.contract	Contract jobs, San Francisco Bay area, California
ba.jobs.misc	Discussions about jobs in San Francisco
ba.jobs.offered	Positions offered in San Francisco
ba.jobs.resumes	Resumes of job seekers in San Francisco
bionet.jobs	Job openings in the biological sciences
bionet.jobs.wanted	Persons looking for job opportunities in biological fields
misc.jobs.misc	Discussions about jobs/job hunting
misc.jobs.offered	General positions available
misc.jobs.offered.entry	Entry-level positions available
misc.jobs.contract	Contract positions, usually short-term
misc.jobs.resumes	Post your resume here, ASCII format only
news.lists	News-related statistics and lists
sci.research.careers	Issues relevant to careers in scientific research
umn.cs.jobs	University of Minnesota, Computer Science
umn.general.jobs	General job postings at the University of Minnesota
Veronica	gopher://gopher.scs.unr.edu:70/11/ veronica
Virtual Library (CERN)	http://info.cern.ch/hypertext/ DataSources/bySubject/Overview.html
WebCrawler	http://webcrawler.cs.washington.edu/ WebCrawler/query.html
Whole Internet Catalog	http://nearnet.gnn.com/wic/wics/ index.html/
WWW Worm	http://www.cs.colorado.edu/www
Yahoo	http://home.netscape.com/home/ internet-directory.html
Yahoo List	http://akebono.stanford.edu/yahoo/ Business/Employment/

Bibliography of Suggested Readings

The following is a bibliography of resources that have been mentioned throughout this volume. At the end of each listing is the name of each author who cited the particular source. This list would be helpful for further reading on current trends, and would also be helpful for collection development purposes.

Bellovin, Steven and Cheswick, William. *Firewalls and Internet Security: Repelling the Wily Hacker.* Addison-Wesley Publishing Co., 1994. (Iaccarino)

Bridges, William. *JobShift: How to Prosper in a Workplace Without Jobs.* Addison-Wesley Publishing Co., 1994. (Willdorf)

Directory of Electronic Journals, Newsletters, and Academic Discussion Lists. 4th ed. Washington, DC: Association of Research Libraries, 1994. (updated annually) (Riley, Anderson)

Engle, Mary, et al. *Internet Connections: A Librarian's Guide to Dial Up Access and Use.* American Library Association, 1993. (Berkowitz/Brodie)

Franklin, John & Smith, Elizabeth. *Job Hunting With Your PC.* Alpha Books, 1992. (Lorenzen)

Gonyea, James C. *The On-Line Job Search Companion: A Complete Guide to Hundreds of Career Planning Job Resources Available Via Your Computer.* McGraw-Hill, 1994. (Lorenzen)

Hahn, Harley. *The Internet Complete Reference.* Osborne McGraw-Hill, 1994. (Berkowitz/Brodie)

Hahn, Harley. *The Internet Yellow Pages.* Osborne McGraw-Hill, 1994. (Berkowitz/Brodie)

Kennedy, Joyce L. & Morrow, Thomas J. *Electronic Job Search Revolution: Win with the New Technology That's Reshaping Today's Job Market.* John Wiley & Sons, 1993. (Lorenzen)

Kennedy, Joyce L. & Morrow, Thomas J. *Electronic Resume Revolution: Create a Winning Resume for the New World of Job Seeking.* John Wiley & Sons, 1993. (Lorenzen)

[Haworth co-indexing entry note]: "Bibliography of Suggested Readings." Co-published simultaneously in *The Reference Librarian* (The Haworth Press, Inc.) No. 55, 1996, pp. 119-120; and: *Career Planning and Job Searching in the Information Age* (ed: Elizabeth A. Lorenzen) The Haworth Press, Inc., 1996, pp. 119-120. Single or multiple copies of this article are available from The Haworth Document Delivery Service [1-800-342-9678, 9:00 a.m. - 5:00 p.m. (EST). E-mail address: getinfo@ haworth.com].

Krol, Ed. *The Whole Internet User's Guide & Catalog.* O'Reilly & Associates, 1994. (Berkowitz/Brodie)

Valauskas, John and Nancy R. *The Internet Troubleshooter: Help for the Logged-On and Lost.* American Library Association, 1994. (Berkowitz/Brodie)

Weddle, Peter D. *Electronic Resumes for the New Job Market: Resumes That Work for You Twenty-Four Hours a Day.* Impact Publishers, 1995. (Lorenzen)

For Product Safety Concerns and Information please contact our EU representative GPSR@taylorandfrancis.com / Taylor & Francis Verlag GmbH, Kaufingerstraße 24, 80331 München, Germany

T - #0026 - 230425 - C0 - 229/152/7 [9] - CB - 9781560248385 - Gloss Lamination